The High-Tech Product Manager's Survival Guide

Dennis Blanco

ISBN: **1508791384**
ISBN 13: **978-1508791386**

Contents

Introduction

Congratulations on becoming a Product Manager. You have embarked on a wonderful journey with limitless possibilities in your career. Product Management may be a stepping-stone to advancing to the executive ranks or to Sales or Marketing. In and of itself, Product Management offers a unique perspective on the business.

Whether you came from the technical or business side of the house, your reasons for becoming a Product Manager may include money, exposure to the business side, visibility among executives, upward mobility, customer exposure, or having outgrown your current role.

The type of company we discuss in this book is one that primarily sells IT products. This company operates a business-to-business (B2B) selling model both direct and channel oriented types.

A B2B company primarily sells to other businesses. A B2B company's customer or end user may be another B2B provider or a B2C (business-to-consumer) provider, i.e., one that sells to an individual user. For example, Oracle, as a B2B company, may sell to another B2B company, such as Avaya, or to a B2C company, such as American Express.

We exclude retail and purely web-based models, as the mechanics of Product Management differ significantly in those markets. There are companies that operate both B2B and B2C models, such as Microsoft, Apple, Dell, and others. For these companies, we focus on the B2B aspect of their business. We exclude Manufacturing, as well as pure professional service-oriented businesses for the same reasons. The reference for the company's model is the high-tech industry borne of the Silicon Valley experience.

What Do We Mean by Product Management?

Here are some industry definitions of Product Management that will serve our purpose:

The organizational structure within business that manages the development, marketing, and sale of a product (or set of products) throughout the product's life cycle. It encompasses the broad set of activities required to get the product to market and support it thereafter.[1]

Product Management is an organizational life-cycle function within a company dealing with the planning, forecasting, or marketing of a product or products at all stages of the product life cycle.[2]

The core definition includes *management of products through their life cycles*.

To this end, Product Management is not the process of collecting and using data on the products that a business or organization sells, handles, or makes.[3]

Anything to do with pure marketing, such as marketing communications, PR, competitive analysis, channel communications, website and social-media management, and the like is excluded from our definition.

The Product-Management Model

Let us say a few things about where the Product-Management function fits into an organization. In the industry, roughly 75 percent of companies have Product Management reporting to Marketing, and the rest typically report to Engineering.

In a small number of cases, Product Management may be its own business unit and, therefore, under its own executive. In theory, this model is devoid of misguided loyalty and solely focused on what is good for the business overall. Product Management's orientation will then depend on compensation.

---

[1] "Product Management," *BusinessDictionary.com*, accessed June 14, 2015, http://www.businessdictionary.com/definition/product-management.html#ixzz2e983wJ2F.

[2] "Product Management," *Wikipedia*, accessed June 14, 2015, http://en.wikipedia.org/wiki/Product_management.

[3] "Product Management," *techopedia*, accessed June 14, 2015, http://www.techopedia.com/definition/28371/product-management.

Under no circumstances should Product Management report to Sales. In this model, Product Management is very tactical and will have ever-changing product requirements to the point that the Product Manager will lose credibility with Engineering. Sales' point of view is too short-term for Product Management. Product Management takes the longer-term, strategic perspective in order to be effective.

We can tie a Product-Management model to the maturity of a company. In a start-up, it usually reports to Engineering. In this model, the Product Managers are very technical and very hands-on when it comes to product features. At this stage of the company's life cycle, there are relatively few objectives (primarily, get the release out ASAP) and few conflicting requirements (whatever the lead customer wants, he gets).

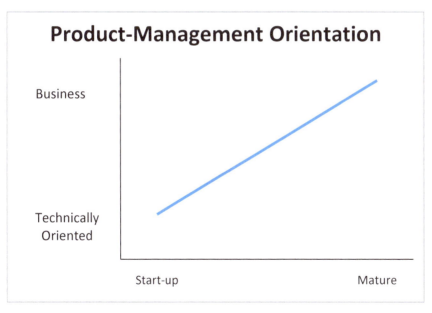

Figure 1. A company's maturity may indicate how Product Management is oriented.

As the company matures, the emphasis on product management's role moves from technical to business oriented. When a company leaves the start-up or small-company mode for a large, established–company mode, there will be a greater emphasis on Sales and

Marketing, requiring Product Management to become oriented to that side of the company. Few exceptions are found at the low end (small company and business oriented), but there are plenty of examples at the top end (large, mature company and Engineering oriented).

Much also depends on the orientation of the company: Sales, Engineering, Operations, Finance, and others. As the company matures and becomes more focused on Sales and Marketing, Product Management must broaden its perspective. It becomes an asset of the business side. It means less involvement with the technical aspects of the product and more emphasis on business strategy and selling. Often, the required skill set shifts from detail-oriented technical Product Management to a detail-oriented business manager.

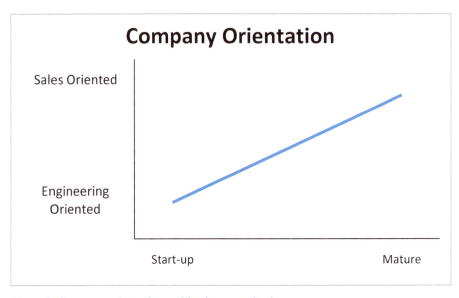

Figure 2. Company orientation and business emphasis.

The company's orientation is a sign of its strategic direction. As a start-up (or in bootstrapping mode), it is typically Engineering oriented. This is because the focus is on creating a solid product and pleasing the relatively small customer base. For a start-up, this could be a single customer. Therefore, focus is important, because all the eggs are in one basket. There are large companies (e.g., Apple, Google) that maintain their Engineering orientation and are still very effective and financially viable.

This is because they continue to innovate at a pace that surpasses market expectations and have become known for innovation. Note that these are B2C high-tech companies. Although the model works for a B2B high-tech company (SAP and Siemens), it is more difficult to sustain. B2B products are more complex and costly, and the life-cycle expectations are night and day compared to consumer products where the turnover rate is measured in months, not years.

Typically, a B2B company focused on growth will be Sales oriented. This company is intent on new customers and increasing market share. For Product Management, this means that the ties between product and profit have to be clearer and more tangible. There is more accountability on Product Management to demonstrate (or at least model in a convincing way) revenue for a given feature.

A company may become Operations or Services oriented when it wants to maintain a stable customer base. Although interested in new business and growth, the company protects the existing base as its golden goose. It focuses attention on repeatability and optimized delivery processes. It minimizes risk at the back end. For Product Management, this means more attention is paid to processes. The primary goal is to ensure that product and delivery processes are well synchronized.

When a company is in trouble, it becomes Finance oriented. This model is not viable for innovation, growth, or market stability. Handing the company reins over to Finance means that investments necessary for innovation and growth will be stifled. This model cannot be sustained in the long run and must have a logical end: the company is sold, goes under, or comes out of its slump and begins investing again. For Product Management, this implies conservatism for tactical activities and true vision when it comes to strategic initiatives. If the premise is that the company will come out of its slump intact, then Product Management must prepare the product for future growth while maintaining its revenue stream and viability in the market in the short run.

The Spectrum

We can view the range of jobs within a typical high-tech company as a spectrum, with Sales on one end and Engineering on the other. Product Management sits in the middle. Figure 3 shows the spectrum of roles surrounding Product Management.

Figure 3. The spectrum of roles surrounding Product Management.

As we move from left to right, the drivers of each role migrate from that of purely revenue to that of purely technical. Motivation moves from purely monetary and the thrill of the chase to technical achievement and the ability to create. Everyone craves recognition but differs in the nature of that recognition. Sales are motivated and recognized for achieving quota. The compensation plan controls Sales' behavior. Engineers are recognized for innovation. Product direction and technical merit modulate Engineers' behavior.

Sales thrive on dealing with different people and meeting new people regularly. Engineers generally prefer a stable and known environment. Sales are fine with the ambiguities and dynamic nature of the job and understand that an individual's perception is truth; whereas Engineers prefer solid, unambiguous, and objective facts.

Product Management is in between. A good Product Manager will embody characteristics from both sides and take the best that each point of view has to offer. Product Management exists so that these two worlds do not collide.

The Hats You Wear

As a Product Manager, you will be required to wear many hats. People say this of their roles all the time, but it is no truer than as a Product Manager.

When I became a Product Manager, I thought of my role as being a silo. I saw myself as being smack in the middle between Engineering and Sales with a specific role to fill. However, there are other functions between those two roles, and the Product Manager spans that spectrum rather than being a single part of it. Depending on whom you ask, the Product Manager can be an extension of Engineering or an extension of Marketing or even Sales.

The impression you leave on your peers and management largely determines your success as a Product Manager. It is a very visible position—sometimes for the wrong reasons. Much of your success is determined by the level of confidence others have in your ability to make the right decisions as a Product Manager. Another way of ensuring this confidence is by showing your flexibility in managing the different roles you will have to play.

In any case, you have to decide where Product Management sits in your organization (closer to Sales or Engineering), where your personal preferences are, and where your boss wants you to be. Wearing different hats is not an option for you; it is expected.

This Book

This book is organized into five parts.

Part 1 is about the job itself. Although there are different ways that an organization may define your job, there are foundational elements of every high-tech Product Manager's position, without which you are not really a Product Manager.

Part 2 is about your relationships. We will discuss the relationships you build and how to improve upon them. We will also cover some dos and don'ts when it comes to relationships.

Part 3 is on the business side. Once you know your job, you turn your attention to understanding how the business side works. This is a critical success factor for the Product Manager because, at the end of the day, he or she will be measured on the success of the business.

Part 4 contains some useful tips and tricks of getting through the day. Even if Product Management is a big trash can, it doesn't mean your day has to be that messy.

Part 5 is about your career. We will discuss how to look out for you and how to position yourself for marketability and upward mobility.

The temptation is to focus on the Product Manager's inward-facing job, such as requirements writing, product life-cycle management, market research, customer advocacy, and the like. By discussing outward-facing tasks—including field enablement, product marketing, maintaining customer relationships, and so on, as well as daily tactical and career-strategic objectives—we approach the function of Product Management more completely. This is what some may call "*whole*" Product Management.

Throughout, we will follow two fictional, high-tech Product Managers and observe how they embody the principles discussed here—or not. Our two Product Managers come from different backgrounds and became Product Managers for their own reasons. They also work for companies that differ in the product types they sell, but as we will see, they will encounter similar challenges.

As we will see, they cover different parts of the spectrum. It is difficult to imagine someone who can span the entire spectrum and do a decent job of it. Even within these comfort zones, we will see how far outside their job descriptions these two Product Managers have to go to get the job done.

Although both Product Managers will be called upon to work across and beyond their comfort zones, each may have a tendency to stay within a comfort zone. Regardless of your tendency to be on one side of the spectrum or another, the most effective strategy is to strive to make the elements of a Product Manager central in your objectives.

This doesn't mean it has to be in the middle of your comfort zone, but do keep in mind that the Product Manager is supposed to strike a balance between being completely Engineering oriented and completely Sales oriented.

Part 1: Your Job

Meet Sue and James

The landing was shaky at Las Vegas McCarran International Airport. As the Boeing B-737 banked across the hills at Sloan Canyon National Conservation Area, it bobbled like the sudden first drop of a roller coaster. Some fool behind James shrieked, "Woo-hoo. Let's do that again!"

James's stomach was still in his throat when he walked onto the concourse. The sounds and smells of Vegas assaulted him. There was the familiar ding-dong of the slot machines perched right outside the gates. The designated smoking rooms could not contain the smell. Oddly enough, nearby was an oxygen bar, with its bubbling Plexiglas tubes, which puzzled him.

"Five," he thought as he walked toward the trams that would take him to the terminal. A ten-times-larger-than-life Tiger Woods smiled down at him, surrounded by other glittering advertisements filled with empty promises of the high life. This was his fifth time in Sin City this year. He zipped past the baggage conveyors, smirking at the silly passengers waiting for their checked luggage. Did they realize it would take eons to get their bags? He walked past them toward the cab line.

One flight ahead of James, Sue tried to figure out why the cab ride from the airport seemed to take forever when she could see the convention center from the airport. She felt she could walk there. The driver was giving her tips on betting on the boxing match that night. She did not know what to say, except to politely thank him while wishing he would shut up. It took nearly twenty minutes to reach the hotel and convention center, although the traffic was light.

As soon as Sue checked in, she ran to her room and accessed the Wi-Fi before unpacking her suitcase, which she had left by the door. She had written a dozen e-mails on the plane and was anxious to send them off. There was Wi-Fi on the plane, but she thought the fee was ridiculous. When the e-mails were safely buzzing across cyberspace at light speed, she looked around. The room was a reminder of why she did not like to travel.

The décor was bright and garish. Like the rest of Vegas, it assaulted the senses and kept one in a perpetual dream world with no tomorrow or yesterday. Responsibilities, like jobs and mortgages, were a vague memory. Everything was designed to separate you from your money. Sue decided to go down and check out the conference. Registration was already open.

The cheerful bottle blonde behind the counter handed James his badge and a blue, reusable grocery bag bearing several sponsors' logos. Inevitably, it was filled with a conference agenda, proceedings, and Marketing collateral from companies who did not have enough budget for a banner or a booth. He thanked her and forced a smile. It was hard to be cheerful when doing the same thing five times in six months.

James felt like he had lost a bet—to his boss. Lauren had put a training item as part of his Management by Objectives (MBO) and he had been stalling on this one all year. After reminding him so many times, she had finally signed him up for a Product-Management Conference in Vegas in her cheerful but final way.

Sue bumped into James as he was giving his fake smile. They exchanged curt apologies and moved on. She noted that he was better dressed than most of the other delegates. "In fact, he would be striking even in a crowd of salespeople," she thought. Maybe this conference was not just for Product Managers. He was more GQ than *Men's World*. She labeled him one of the MBA-type Product Managers, as opposed to the Engineer-type, like her.

Sue got her bag of conference junk and hurried back to her room. There were tons of e-mails to go through, and no time at all to dawdle. She noticed there was a cocktail hour that night as a welcome reception for the delegates. She dismissed it at first, wondering what was on the room-service menu. By the time she got back to her room, she decided it might be better to suffer the welcome reception and get halfway decent food instead of what she always imagined were leftovers for someone dumb enough to order room service and pay those prices. The reception surely would be no better than heavy hors d'oeuvres, but it was free, and there would be drinks. Just the thing that might take the edge off. Anyway, there was time to change her mind again later. For now, there was an in-box waiting.

James hung around the conference area for a bit. He took note of the companies going into the exhibit hall to set up. He could see that they were mostly consulting companies, recruiters, third-party software developers, and Microsoft. No doubt, some were more interested in recruiting than they were in helping. The United States is still the biggest owner of software intellectual property. Many of those setting up were companies based in India, China, and Vietnam—all outsourcers hoping to get a piece of the action. Outsourcing software development is not as easy as outsourcing chip manufacturing, call centers, tech support, and the steel industry. Although other countries have competent universities, the United States is still on the leading edge of software development.

When James had made up his mind about how the exhibit hall conversations would go, he wandered off to see the rest of the convention center. It was not to familiarize himself—he had been at this one twice before—but to see how busy it was. He poked around at a few of the ridiculously priced shops, had lunch at a café, played some slots, and even wandered into a bookstore—all to avoid going back to the desolation of his room. He opted instead to answer a few e-mails that seemed urgent on his smartphone. He made some calls and tried to do most of his business amid the vacationers waiting to rid themselves of their hard-earned cash. Cocktail hour could not come soon enough. But then came an urgent e-mail from the field. A sales guy from the Northeast was about to blow a gasket unless

James responded to an urgent e-mail asking for documentation and a presentation. He trudged back to his room. He was going to climb Mt. Outlook after all.

After what seemed like minutes but was actually three hours, Sue finally looked up from her screen and at the alarm clock on the nightstand. She remembered the cocktail reception, and, although not a big drinker, she needed to eat. She had had nothing since breakfast.

It was early when Sue got to the ballroom, yet the place was nearly full. People gravitated to the bar mostly, so there was no waiting at the buffet. She piled up on the heavy hors d'oeuvres, grabbed a bottle of water, and found an empty table. She pulled out her smartphone and started to work.

"You mind if I sit here?" It was GQ, carrying a plate and a drink. He was motioning two chairs away from Sue. He did not really need to ask, as it was understood, in these settings, that all seats were free-for-all, but it was a way of starting a conversation.

She decided she would be sociable. After all, that is what the reception was all about. She smiled and waved her hand at the chair, telling him to sit. She did not have to break the ice, because James was a natural at that.

"Do you remember a time when mobile phones were getting smaller?" he asked, pointing at her smartphone, which was the latest from Korea.

Sue looked down at her gadget, which was so large it could not be holstered and so powerful it rivaled many desktop PCs. She had to admit that they were getting ridiculously large now. She smiled and replied, "No, I'm too young to remember those old days."

James laughed. They were no more than a year apart, and both knew it. "What's wrong with one of these?" he asked, pulling out a slim smartphone that was not as smart as hers. "It actually works great— as a phone!"

"It takes a secure guy to carry around one of those," Sue said, arching an eyebrow.

"I'll take that as a compliment," he said while taking a bite of some tapas from his plate and sipping his Cabernet.

"So, what brought you to this thing?" she asked.

"My boss railroaded me into it," said James. He was surprised to hear himself being so candid. Normally he would have given some politically correct answer and tried to spin some yarn about how good the convention would be. This time he decided that honesty wasn't going to hurt him.

"Me too," she said. "He told me I needed to get out of the office and that this would be my training MBO."

"Yeah, that's what Lauren said, too. I'm out of the office so much you'd think she'd want to keep me there for a change. Maybe they don't like me to be in the office, so they keep sending me away." He winked and held out his hand. "I'm James Herrera."

"Sue Lam," she said.

Introductions were superfluous, being that their names were printed in seventy-two–point font on oversized badges hanging from their necks. Anywhere else and they would have seemed like idiots, but somehow, in such a weird place with the same kind of people they worked with, it was appropriate.

The conversation naturally drifted to the conference agenda. They compared tracks that were neatly printed on the back of their giant name tags. It turned out that they signed up for the same ones.

The topics they picked?

- Pop, Sizzle, and Zing: How to Write Requirements
- Talking Turkey: Effective Communication in the Age of Social Media
- The Market Isn't Ready, But It Will Be Soon
- The Inmates Have Taken Over the Asylum
- I'm Not the Sales Engineer

They made more small talk until their electronics buzzed and beeped for attention. Then they drifted off. James excused himself first to say good night to his wife, and Sue got an urgent call from the QA testers working into the night. She ran back to her room to log in.

What Is Your Job?

The following are harsh statements, but they are no less true.

If Sales ran product development, the company would have a different product for every customer and a dedicated support person who practically lives at the customer's site. Sales does not look backward or forward. They live in the moment and do not want to be bothered by the customer again unless he is buying something new. They close the deal in as little time as possible and move on.

If Engineering ran the company, they would tell the customer to hang on until the product was perfect and that it would be worth the wait because they would never need patches or have to call for tech support. There would be one product to fit all possible customers and customer needs forever. However, the product would never see the light of day. Engineering wants completeness. They have to cover every corner case because they do not want to have to revisit that version after release. They may behave as if hampered by neither time nor money. They are innovating, after all.

This is why you, the Product Manager, are needed. You are the balance between never releasing a product and releasing it before it's ready, between a product that is too specific to a very small number of customers and one that is not fit for purpose, between making money and losing market share, between an unreasonable amount of bug fixes and not keeping up with the competition. You are the translator of market requirements and the gatekeeper of priorities. You have Profit-and-Loss (P&L) responsibility, whether the boss tells you explicitly or not.

Your *Raison d'Être*

Product requirements are central to your role. You will get requirements in the form of:

- cryptic e-mails from sales
- dictated one-liners from your boss as he passes you in the hallway
- expensive market reports thrown at you by the marketing VP
- an old list from the person who used to have your job
- Post-it notes left on your monitor by anonymous
- support tickets that miraculously appear in your in-box with you as "prime"

Of course, there should be a formal product-request process that is supposed to keep these to a minimum. Sooner or later, you will have to collate these, research them, prioritize them, and translate them into something Engineering can design. Engineering, of course, will not accept anything less than the agreed-upon Product Requirements Document (PRD) template, which may have been agreed upon by someone other than you (and you realize that none of your Product Management peers agreed to it either). Usually, this is a formal document.

The document is the last piece in a complicated puzzle. By the time you get it done, everyone, including Engineering, already knows what is in it. You get there by way of the spreadsheet, which, next to having your own personal project-manager assistant, is the best method of tracking and prioritizing requirements. Unless you want to have triple-digit releases of your PRD, it is practical to employ the spreadsheet.

Despite the formal process, different groups will still use the aforementioned informal methods because it suits them. Regardless of how rigid your organization is about formality in the request process, you still have to consider the ones that come in from an unsanctioned channel, because they might be valid requests. You will go through the same process of vetting the request, assigning a business case to it, running revenue projections, and prioritizing the different requests.

The essence of a business case is the amount of revenue you expect to make if the company chooses to invest in a new product or feature. Some key elements are Total Addressable Market (TAM), Sales pipeline, and key customers. You may also be required to provide elements related to opportunity cost such as competitive disadvantage, impact to installed base, and strategic impact. The revenue may be broken down by year, region of the world, product, and an aggregate over a set number of years (used to calculate the Return on Investment (ROI)).

Bigger projects require separate business cases, including analyst projections and past performance of the market and the company. Smaller projects or features may only require a short paragraph or bullet points on a slide. In either case, you should be well versed in the business case of each item you request and be ready to defend it at any given moment.

The first order of business is to document the request. Whether for a major release, a service pack, or a minor release, you will likely have leftover requirements—ones that were too big for the last release or fell too far below the line.

Rarely will you be starting from scratch, unless it is a completely new product. The key to documenting the request is to take a narrow view and strive to understand the request as if it were the only requirement of that product. It will be tempting to prioritize it according to what is already there, but that could be detrimental.

When you look at a request as if it were the only requirement, you will understand how it relates to the business, and you will be better able to ask the right questions regarding its business case. You will be less likely to assume you know the nature of the request and how similar it is to others that have preceded it. You will be less likely to dismiss it offhand. You will be more likely to look into it in more detail and give the request its due.

Viewing a request with this sort of tunnel vision opens up your mind to possibilities that may not have occurred to you to that point and perhaps gives you a different point of view. This process will likely be more time-consuming but may lead to that gold nugget of a requirement from which your next killer app springs forth. Isn't that worth taking some more time to understand the requirement?

Once you have understood, documented, and articulated each requirement, the mundane job of prioritizing them comes next. The spreadsheet paradigm is easiest because you can move requirements around easily. There are many ways of prioritizing.

Ideally, a business case—or even better, a sales pipeline—exists to justify putting a higher priority on certain requirements. A strategic business case is also good enough (i.e., if the requirement opens up a new market, positions the company for larger market share, or keeps the competition at bay); these are good strategic reasons to prioritize a requirement high even when the business case is soft.

Some bad reasons for prioritizing a requirement are:

- The sales guy thinks he can sell it to one customer.
- It would look cool.
- You've always wanted a product with one of these.
- Engineering says it can do it for no cost.
- It has been on the list for so long.
- The other Product Managers are putting one in their product.
- The VP thinks it is a good idea.
- The competition has it, and so on.

There is, of course, a gray area where a requirement might fall, and you have to decide how high to prioritize it. Some of these might be strategic-customer requirement, market-niche requirement, technology improvement, and so on.

Sometimes the gray area is the place where you spend most of your time deciding. This is OK because it forces you to scrutinize the requirement, and should it make it to your priority list, it means you found a way to tie it to a business case.

The Right Way to Write Your Requirements

You are the business owner and not the Business Analyst or Architect who works for Engineering. Act like a business owner. Do not concern yourself with *how* to design something, rather be concerned about *what* you want it to look like.

Once you have assigned a business case to each requirement, you can begin the task of prioritizing them. The spreadsheet paradigm is the most efficient method, as it allows you to create a summary view of each requirement, including headings like:

- Title
- Description
- Business Case
- Source
- Release Vehicle
- Region
- Market
- Strategic Customer
- Business Impact

The advantage is that you can move the columns around en masse. Adding a column for "Notes" or "Comments" gives you a flexible, free-form, and unstructured field to use.

Regardless of how you prioritize the requirements, they should fall into three main categories: Must-Have, Nice to Have, and Who Cares. There are many ways of categorizing requirements, and inevitably, you will be forced to use a methodology that your Engineering team understands and is willing to abide by. The bottom line is that these three categories should form the foundation for any method of prioritization you use.

The advantage of these three categories is that they do not inherently mean the requirement is in or out. The litmus test for each is the particular market, business case, or product strategy behind the requirement.

A Must-Have means that, no matter what, it is required in the next release. A solid line should be drawn under the last Must-Have requirement. You should be able to articulate the business case for each Must-Have, whether it is strategic, revenue, or market share. You must be able to stand in front of Engineering and, under no circumstances, budge on these requirements. Must-Haves ideally comprise a small minority of your list. This is because the Must-Haves will require the greatest amount of resources (time, head count, expense) and will be completed at the expense of the rest of the list. If the Must-Haves do not meet these criteria, then, they are Nice to Haves.

A Nice to Have is the middle of the road. From your perspective, Engineering can work this list (in the priority order you have chosen) once they have exhausted (i.e., designed) the Must-Haves. The majority of your requirements ideally fall into this category. The business cases for these requirements may be a little more nebulous but still valid. This list may comprise tangible benefits but may not have an easily measurable impact on revenue. The Nice-to-Have requirement could easily fall into a Must-Have if a solid business case emerges, so Nice to Haves should get attention from Engineering. Similarly, Nice to Haves may fall into the Who-Cares category if the benefits evaporate.

A Who Cares means you have documented the requirements, and they may mean something to someone, but you can neither find a compelling business case nor articulate a large enough business impact. You want Engineering to be aware of these requirements while also allowing them to be ignored.

Beware the requirement sourced by Engineering. Engineers are supposed to be creative. They also feel ownership of the product, and you must respect this parent-baby relationship. From time to time, Engineering will propose requirements that they deem to have business value.

As the business owner, you have to put them through the same litmus test you would a requirement that comes from the field. There is a political component in that you have to be careful not to dismiss a requirement too quickly, as it may damage your relationship with

Engineering. At the same time, you have to remember that you will need to justify the requirement to your management and the company's senior management. "It was Engineering's idea" is not an acceptable justification or a good place to hide.

Begin with the End in Mind

Write the press release first. It helps focus your attention on what is important to the market. Remember, you are using up dozens or even hundreds of staff years to develop the product. If the press release is a dud, is it really worth all that effort?

> New City, USA—Tech Company Inc., a leading provider of technologically advanced products, announced today the release of Blue Sky v2.2, its flagship platform. Blue Sky v2.2 builds upon the vast market share that this advanced platform introduced. This new product will continue to take market share away from competitors due to its better integration, flexibility, and mobility. Blue Sky's small footprint ensures portability, and its power will provide customers with the most advanced platform available today.

Now, each product release does not have to be groundbreaking or game changing, but it is better if you write the press release as if it were. The PR, after all, is a Marketing tool designed to extol the virtues of the product and highlight the most compelling features. It is usually a set of buzzwords aimed at search engines, prospects, and analysts. The PR is not product documentation; it is a piece of advertisement.

Yet, within the acronyms and buzzwords, should lie the solid foundation on which you, the Product Manager, have built your requirements and the strategy for the product. Beginning with the end in mind helps keep those things top of mind.

The Circle of Product Life

Like it or not, the Product Manager is the keeper of a product's life cycle. Higher authorities may make end-of-life decisions, but the Product Manager nurtures the product from inception to end of life. Like organic life-forms, the high-tech product has infancy, youth, adulthood, and maturity.

It is not often that a single Product Manager sees a product from beginning to end. No matter at what stage you take responsibility for a product, take the perspective that you will be there until the product's end of life. This will enable you to take the larger and longer perspective when it comes to writing requirements.

Each cycle of requirements presents an opportunity to ensure that the product has continuity from one release to the next. Often the Product Manager starts with an inside-out perspective. Requirements may start out with the noblest intentions: adoption of a new and exciting technology, employment of a popular new design process, integration of a newly acquired company, scalability, portability, supportability—the list goes on. Too often, however, the customer perspective takes a lower priority or is ignored altogether. The customer does not care about new technology if it means the upgrade path is costly for him. A new design process means nothing to the customer if the result is that his feature request takes several years to materialize. The customer will not appreciate the integration of an acquired company if his version of the product leaves him stranded with no migration path.

The customer simply wants the product to work. He wants upgrades to be worry-free. He wants expansions to be at minimal cost. He wants his favorite features to persist from one release to the next. New features should be easy to learn. New releases should be better quality than the last and few and far between. After all, we are talking about enterprise class technology, not consumer electronics, such as iPhones.

The Product Manager who takes the customer's perspective when writing requirements will produce a more balanced set of requirements that meets market demands and preserves continuity from one release to the next. The result serves both masters, the installed base and new customers.

Working Outside the Box

At some point, you will be called upon to go out of your comfort zone and totally outside your job description. Whether this call is literal (such as your boss telling you) or implied (someone volunteers you by inference), you will probably feel there is no choice—no one else to do it.

Whatever the reason, you feel compelled to do it. Sometimes it is not enough to think outside the box; you have to work outside it. You will have to rewrite the rules or invent new ones. It is truly blazing a new trail.

In these cases, your creativity is your best tool. That out-of-box thinking we've all claimed from time to time will now be put into play. This situation can arise in a number of ways and will be your opportunity to shine.

People are often afraid when their manager presents them with an opportunity—and for good reason. Usually it is some scut work that the manager himself does not want to do, or someone who did not want to do it has thrown it to him hot-potato style. You become the fool who ends up doing it because, well, you do not have anyone else to toss it to. No wonder people hate so-called opportunities.

On the other hand, it may not pay to jump on every gap-filling task that comes your way. There will be many of these opportunities, so be judicious about which ones you take on. Measure the risk-reward ratio of the opportunity. Who is likely to be viewing the results? If the answer is somewhere between your VP and the CEO, it is worth considering; even if it involves sweeping the dust from underneath the file cabinets. You cannot afford to miss such a career-making opportunity. However, do consider the risks involved in failure. Nothing is ever assured, but, if the task has no upside or is doomed to fail, the visibility may do you more harm than good. It will pay to have a trusted advisor within the company.

Some opportunities are harder to characterize. Yes, it may or may not be visible to the CEO, but it may also mean goodwill with Sales. It could cause someone who is important to your work to owe you one. This is a tough call because an out-of-box opportunity could consume your time. Only you can judge for sure.

Part 2: Your Relationships

Much of this section is devoted to your relationship with Engineers. This is because the majority of your relationship building will be with the R&D organization. We will discuss your relationships with other disciplines, particularly Sales, in the next section.

James went into the office late on Monday. The baby was up all night it seemed, and he took turns with Ellie trying to get him back to sleep. He was teething, and there was not a lot they could do. Fortunately Julia, the four-year-old, slept through it all.

He stopped for a latte and a muffin, so he was somewhat alert by the time he walked in. It was a good thing, because he had barely put his laptop case on the desk when he was barraged with, "Where have you been?" and, "Did you forget today is Build Day? We were here at the crack of dawn, and things aren't going well."

"Of course things aren't going well," he thought. "That's why we have this day built into the process—to iron out the kinks."

Moondoggie's software-validation process had a two-step regression built into it. The first one was part of the formal quality-assurance process, and the second one was part of the build process.

Build Day was a misnomer, as the objective was the final regression and the final build, all on the same day. In the three years that James had been working for the company, Build Day had never lasted less than a week. Someone in Engineering once suggested they change the name to Build Week or The Day That Never Ends, but it hadn't stuck. Too much history, or, James thought, "Everyone in Engineering had the illusion that someday they could actually do it in a day."

So today was not build day, it was the first day of Build Day. Lior Noah was the team lead who showed up at the drop of James's

29

briefcase to tell him the bad news. Lior was a compact man who vibrated with nervous energy and looked at James with expectant eyes, waiting for a bit of wisdom from the Product Manager.

"The build didn't happen, James," he said. "All the phase-two tests passed. I don't understand it."

"Did we address the race condition in the scheduling blocks?" James asked, starting up his laptop.

"Of course we did. That was the number-one priority last week."

"What about the network interface locking up?"

"Firmware problem. Christy and Dave took care of that over the weekend."

"Whatever happened to the UI crashing?"

"That's minor. Shouldn't be affecting the build, unless…" Lior paused and looked away. "You might have something there. We commented out that section of code last week. Might explain why the tests passed. I wonder if Eddie ever fixed the problem." He walked away while mumbling to himself.

"Third time's a charm," James thought. He was happy to get Lior going, although he was sure that would turn out not to be the problem. Lior's team was some of the best he had ever worked with.

Sometimes they just needed a wall to bounce things off. And bounce they did. James found himself more of a counselor than a Product Manager on some days. He knew this week was a key week for Engineering. Everyone was watching them. There was anticipation of the build coming out so that they could hit a release date that had already slipped several months.

James knew that if they hit the date, which was that Friday, Engineering would take a bow for it, and the company would laud them as heroes. He also knew that if it did not happen, Sales would turn evil eyes at him and scream for his head on a platter.

"And it's only 9:05," he mumbled after Lior.

Know Your R&D Organization

It pays to understand what makes the Engineering organization tick. This entails knowing the R&D organization from two perspectives: how they are supposed to do their jobs and how the individuals like to do their jobs.

The first is about the processes they follow. Whether the organization uses an **Agile** process or a conventional waterfall process, there is still a process—and Engineers love to follow a defined path. Knowing how their particular process works will help you understand and relate to each team or individual so that you can navigate the bureaucracy effectively.

Yes, bureaucracy in Engineering. This should come as no surprise. Aren't they, after all, made up of people? Don't some of those people have more ego than others? Aren't some driven by an agenda that is their own and may sometimes be in conflict with the greater plan? Aren't Engineering managers compensated for meeting dates, milestones, and revenue targets? Are they not asked to submit budgets? These things are true of any organization within your company, and, therefore, you can bet that, just like other organizations, there is a tendency for Engineering to be driven by forces other than purely creating product.

Dealing with Engineering is an exercise in effective negotiation. Everything is a negotiation with Engineering. It is always a give-and-take dance that has no real end. It simply shifts from one release to the next.

You will not always get what you want, so settle for getting most of what you need. The essence of prioritization keeps you from going insane trying to figure out why Engineering is so lackluster in their acceptance and implementation of your requirements.

The better your negotiation skills, the closer you will get to what you want.

Sue Lam was hard at work under her desk. Her NetAlyzer had failed to connect, and she was convinced it was the Layer-2 switch underneath her desk, not the appliance. She looked at the tangle of wires connected to the switch and wondered how she had allowed it to get that messy. She knew half those wires were not used anymore, yet they were plugged in, and who knew where the other end went.

She ended up unplugging everything and only reconnecting the ones she needed to get the NetAlyzer back online. It worked, and she felt an enormous sense of satisfaction at her troubleshooting abilities. On the other hand, she felt annoyed that she had to do this in the first place. Why couldn't she just set up something in the real lab instead of turning her cube into a pseudo-lab?

As a matter of fact, why was she still acting like an Engineer when she had left that world long ago? Her manager, Joe, was always encouraging her to think of the business first. After all, wasn't that the role of a Product Manager? "No," she would say, if only to herself, "the Product Manager is supposed to be very technical so that she can communicate requirements to Engineers effectively." The main reason for this was to keep a certain level of respect that she had not gone completely to the dark side. She had to keep her reputation as a geek in those circles.

Still, she felt guilty that she had spent the last twenty minutes troubleshooting the NetAlyzer so that she could answer a question from one of the Sales Engineers about multicast traffic. She could have just walked over to one of half a dozen Engineers and asked them. She did not want to bother them with a question that anyone who was technical enough could answer.

* * *

The meeting had been going on for two hours. Sue was convinced Engineering was dragging it out to torture her. Joe and the other directors had walked out after the first hour and left her with the other managers to hash out the problems.

They talked about the drivers that were not working on the new NetAlyzer 5500 for the second hour. The appliance had gone to market three months before and had already sold twice as many units as the previous version, the 5250, in the same amount of time.

One of the first to deploy was a global bank. They already had 120 units turned up, with a plan calling for 250 by the end of the year. Two days after unit 120 was turned up, B2B transactions for three sites stopped completely. It took the bank more than eight hours to recover, at a cost of millions of dollars. They reverted the three sites back to 5250s and were now threatening to replace the rest with the competitor's product.

The team had been debating the wrong things, in her opinion. They seemed to be busy covering for their own departments rather than focusing on the root cause and fixing that. Hardware claimed there was nothing wrong with their CPU subsystem design. Firmware said their code was solid and that no significant changes were made since the last design. OS declared their design was solid and that the problem was not related. Core argued that Firmware had never fixed the race condition they brought up months before but had only masked it. UI was quiet but fueled the fire by agreeing with Core and further questioning whether QA caught it. QA indignantly claimed they had tested and validated the fix, which turned out to be more hardware than firmware.

They were going in circles, but apparently no one could see it. Or maybe they were happy to do it because they didn't have to address the problem. Finally, Support turned to Sue and begged her to say something.

"Guys," she began, sounding irritated, "can we go back to the symptoms? I'm not sure I understand it fully." She understood it completely, having been in endless meetings with Sales, Presales, the partner Sales Engineer, the support Engineer, and the customer's Engineers themselves the past three days. She just wanted to refocus the team back to talking about the same topic.

Tony from Support was happy to oblige. "They turned up the unit in Tokyo at midnight; it ran for about six hours with no issues. They brought it online with the rest of the domain and watched it for another couple of hours. When the next hop, Manila, reached its peak period of the day, Tokyo crashed."

"What time was that?" Sylvia from Core asked.

Tony replied, "8:10 a.m. Tokyo time. They ran system diagnostics, and the only error messages that came out were FW4500s. But when they ran the firmware diagnostics, they were clean!

"They rebooted twice, and each time the unit ran for about eight hours before crashing again. By the time they rebooted Tokyo the second time, Oslo and London had also crashed. They spent the next three days rebooting."

"There's something wrong with Manila then," Eric from Hardware suggested. "It was the next hop."

"What about London and Oslo?" Janice from Firmware came back. "They're several hops from Manila and Tokyo. And at least two from each other, right?"

"Right," Tony answered when no one else said anything. They were going nowhere again, so Sue jumped in.

"What about the US sites?" she asked.

"They never turned them up," Tony said. "New Jersey is a lab, so it's isolated. St. Louis is on its own domain. LA is load balancing their 5250 and 5500, and the 5500's traffic is mirrored."

"So they might as well not be running it," Eric said. "It can't be running hot at all."

"Right. They're not doing capacity testing on it, just apps," Tony said.

"What is LA's next hop?" Sue asked. She got a blank stare back. "No one checked?"

"Hang on," Tony said and went off to one side of the room to call his team.

"Manila," he said dramatically when he came back. Everyone looked relieved at the fact that they had at least completed the circle.

Over the next hour, Sue found herself in the position of mediator. The team would go adrift, and she pulled them back to the main topic of conversation. They would dive into a rathole, and she would have to extricate them. But they were making progress, and she wasn't alone. Some, like Tony the Support Manager, were good leaders and backed her up when they noticed the team going adrift. Some, like Janice the Firmware Architect, were sensitive to the mood of the room, asked encouraging questions, and kept the energy positive.

To her surprise, they actually came out with a plan; not only did it make sense, everyone felt like a contributor, and no one felt they were to blame. Sue observed how tense everyone was at the beginning and how relaxed they were at the end. They had something to take back to management and the customer. They left, patting each other on the back for a job well done.

Except for Sue. No one patted her back, and she had come to expect none. She knew that all they had done was survive to fight another day.

Engineers Are People, Too

Sometimes, when a businessperson walks onto the R&D or Engineering floor, he feels like he is in a bubble. Is it real or perceived, based on some preconceived notion about Engineers? They are introverted. They are intellectuals. They do not give straight answers.

In fact, Engineers are people, too. It is easy to categorize Engineers broadly as anything from anal to arrogant. It is important to remember that they should be treated as individuals.

If you think an Engineer is being too analytic, wanting to drill down into the depths of every item you discuss, learn to appreciate his diligence. After all, isn't that what he is paid to do? If he asks you to dive deep into details, understand that he simply wants to do the most complete job possible.

Most of the time what people interpret as arrogance or avoidance is simply a desire to get the right answer—not to *be* right but to get to the right answer. That is why you will get five levels of "Why is this important?" interrogation.

Develop relationships with Engineers. This goes for any kind of Engineer: design, design support, tech support, etc. You can get a lot of things done off-line and off process if you take the time to develop a good relationship with one or two key people. Remember that Engineers love processes because they are orderly. This does not mean they are incapable of thinking outside the box. Even if they can do something easily out of process, they might throw the process book at you if they decide you are a jerk. They will hide behind process and formality. At some point, you will get into a jam, and escalating will only waste time.

Imagine what you can accomplish if there is one Engineer or Engineering Manager who will turn things around quickly for you or even pick up your cause and fight for it within the organization. Isn't it worth taking an extra few minutes to get to know that person? Isn't this what you normally do when you meet customers or business partners?

Engineering does not like to be taken for granted. If you take the time to make them feel special and not like some cog in a wheel that you, the Product Manager, continually tighten the screws on, you will become more effective at your job. There is, of course, the reality that, no matter what you do, there are some personalities with whom you will get along better than others. Learn these differences, and they will help you navigate the difficult situations.

Some Tension Is Actually Good

There is a school of thought that a certain level of tension is good for productivity. In fact, we see this daily. There is some truth to the aphorism that the squeaky wheel gets the grease. You know some of these squeaky wheels at work, but are they so wrong? Squeaky Wheel applies a lot of tension to the workplace, and the tendency of everyone around him is to apply the grease so that the irritating noise goes away.

If Squeaky were quiet all the time, he would not get anything accomplished—at least not with the same level of expediency he does today. As time goes by, Squeaky manages to keep tension around him, even when he is quiet. This is because the anticipation of the squeak keeps everyone alert. Is that so bad? You can take things to an extreme, but the point is that the right level of tension might be a good thing.

It keeps everyone focused and on task. It keeps the doldrums from seeping in and maintains a sense of urgency, even when there is none. How bad is that? If we treated every nonurgent but important task as if it were urgent, then wouldn't we, in effect, keep things from going into the urgent/important category? This latter is a known killer because the tension that results from it is of the extreme variety.

This implies that a little tension on a constant basis is better than an explosive situation every once in a while. A Project Manager handily uses tension as a weapon on a daily basis. A Project Manager escalates the level of tension simply by being in the room. This is the nature of her job. She must keep everyone on task, because that is what she is measured by at the task level.

I would not suggest you apply the same principle in your role as a Product Manager. Your role is strategic, so you cannot possibly keep the same pace as a Project Manager and expect to be effective in the job you are supposed to do. Apply tension or allow it to rise only at chosen times.

Remember that the reason you are doing it is to add a sense of urgency to something that may not be that urgent at the time but that you know will quickly escalate. You are trying to keep from being hit by the freight train head-on.

Call It What It Is

No matter how diplomatic you may be most of the time, you will find it easier to get through some situations by just calling things what they are, describing the situation as it really is, and simply drawing the obvious conclusion and stating it as plainly as possible. This objectivity has some liberating side effects, such as ending the conversation, keeping everyone from going in circles, and, most importantly, getting everyone to think about the next step.

Why do we fall back on diplomacy, political correctness, or dancing around? It is because we do not want to face certain realities, be called out, or deliver bad news. But who else is going to do it?

Sometimes you have to deliver the bad news to move things along. Continuing to skirt the issue when everyone knows it is there will only prolong the agony. Better for everyone to know the facts and get on with finding a solution to the problem. One of the best compliments I ever received from a Sales Engineer was that I am not afraid to tell it like it is, even when I know the message will not be well received.

The Product Manager's job is not to be popular. It is his job to enable the field to do theirs by arming them with the knowledge they need to sell what they have today.

Transparency is another way of putting it. Decide which things you absolutely must be aboveboard about, and stick to that—no matter what.

My Friend, the Philosopher

A good friend and mentor told me he had two mantras that he always worked by when it came to being a people manager. The first is that "people are all different."

One thing I have learned is that, despite society's attempt to be uniform in almost every way, individuals are truly individual. We all come from differing backgrounds and have unique points of view that are influenced and shaped by our individual experiences.

In any industry or line of business, people tend to be similar in many ways—educational background, social status, and so on. People from the automotive industry have a way of thinking that easily differentiates them from people in the hospitality market. People in high-tech are very obviously different from those in the fashion industry. However, in each industry, there are unique personalities that give rise to diverse social styles, work ethics, learning, and performance.

Ironically, these personalities are probably common across industries. For example, there are the analytical people. They have to study everything before coming to any conclusion. They are concerned with finding the *right* answer. There are the hard-driving people. These people plow forward, sometimes with little thought, and are interested in simply moving things along.

To the extent that you can discover these different types and their needs, you will be able to work better with each individual. Just because George and Jack went to the same school, took the same courses, belong to the same club, and run in the same social circles does not make them the same. They will each have a unique personality that may require you to treat them differently to more effectively work with them.

My friend's second mantra was, "You can't change people." We have certain traits that are hardwired. In the computer world, changing something that is hardwired means you may destroy the computer. As humans, our DNA is hardwired in us. You simply cannot change it without destroying the person.

Some traits are hard-coded. These are the traits that are part of our personality. They have been ingrained from childhood and cannot be changed. These traits, however, can be overridden by other forms of so-called programming. In many cases, we may think these traits have changed, but they have simply been masked.

Part 3: The Business Side

Sales—Your Toughest Customer

Salespeople are hired more for their ability to relate to another individual or group than for their technical knowledge. They learn just enough detail to make themselves credible, but most of that credibility is established minutes after a prospect lays eyes on them.

The successful sales manager inspires trust and confidence by being reliable and helpful. He provides the customer with the necessary technical resources: the Sales Engineer, the support Engineer, and the Product Manager. He provides quotes and collateral, organizes web tutorials, compiles competitive information, and generally makes the customer feel that he will be well taken care of if he buys from the sales manager.

The sales manager is going to be your toughest customer. He is the customer's advocate. He will scrutinize and probe until he gets a satisfactory answer. He will escalate until he gets the feature he needs. He will be a royal pain to the Product Manager. However, if you listen carefully, he can also provide you with some of the best intelligence that can be gathered from the field.

Get to know your sales manager, because this intelligence will not come in one fell swoop. Develop a relationship with him or her. The intel will come over time. You also have to be prepared to have this relationship with many other sales managers so that the information you obtain will not be biased toward a single region or group of customers. Over time, you will learn their language and figure out which bits of drivel are actually nuggets of gold.

A sales manager might say to you that he really needs the square buttons on your user interface to be green. His customer needs them to be green, and this opportunity is worth millions of dollars to the company if only you could make the buttons green. On a different day, the same person is going to insist that the buttons are red because another million-dollar deal rides on those buttons being red. Still another sales manager will want them to be triangular and flashing, and, again, millions of dollars will hang in the balance. At some point, you will have to decide that, if the buttons are important enough to stay in the product, you will probably have to make them configurable.

The point is that, even though salespeople will give you accurate intelligence from the field, it is usually based on a very narrow perspective. It is not their job to look at the landscape; it is yours, and they know it.

Engineers make fun of salespeople or show them disrespect because of their lack of product knowledge. First of all, you do not want your salespeople to have too much depth of knowledge because it will actually get in the way of their salesmanship. That knowledge should end with the sales Engineer. Whenever an Engineer denigrates a salesperson in front of me, I always remind him or her that, if we fired the sales manager today, someone would have to do his job. "And you're my first pick," I would say. That generally ends the conversation.

Sales Engineers Are Tweens

It must be convenient for Sales and Engineering to know that they are on the extreme end of a spectrum. Everyone else is a middle man. Like the Product Manager, the Sales Engineer feels like he has a foot in two different rooms. On one side, he must act like a salesperson. He must be ready to engage in small talk, establish rapport with an individual, and generally provide continuity of engagement. He must also be ready to do the small things the salesperson does, such as quotes and collateral, especially if the customer sees the Sales Engineer and the sales manager as a team. On the other side, he needs to be able to provide the kind of technical expertise and depth required to answer the customer's detailed technical questions. He must do both effectively, because whatever he tells the customer is what will be expected to work. A colleague of mine who is a Sales Engineer likes to say, "Never confuse a good story with the truth."

It will help you to know what the Sales Engineer job entails and how your particular Sales Engineers do their job. At the heart of it all, they need exact technical information that will help them put together a solution that will work for the customer. They are the people with whom you need to share the most bitter and disheartening things about the product with the expectation that they will apply the appropriate filters so that the sale will go through. You will rely on them to figure out which things are important to the customer and which are not. Unlike Sales Managers, Sales Engineers cannot get away with making broad, sweeping statements or assurances that something will work without knowing for sure, because their word will be seen as the company's final word by the customer.

Mea Culpa

At some point, an account will be in deep enough trouble that the customer will insist on talking to the Product Manager. This usually entails meetings with a mixture of technical and business people from the customer's team. This group certainly will influence whether the product stays in-house or not. If that is the case, this is the good news because they are still talking to your company.

The bad news—the reason you are there—is to salvage the account. The reason that the account got to that point may be that the sales team set the wrong expectations about the product, the services team configured the wrong thing, or the support team could not fix the problems, and the customer eventually got fed up with what they perceived to be the runaround. You will, no doubt, have other examples from your own experience. The bottom line is that this did not happen overnight.

It may come down to a fateful meeting with the customer. For days or weeks beforehand, you will be busied out researching the problem, talking to people who will deny their involvement, and explaining the problem to impatient executives who expect you to have an answer yesterday. They will naturally make you nervous. The first thing you have to do is stop thinking about updating your resume.

Expect that the customer is going to get personal. He or she will accuse you of everything, from lying to outright trying to screw him or her. This is normal and has very little to do with everyone's perception of you. To the customer, you are just a name that he has been given as a punching bag. He will take his frustration out on you and make you the focal point of all the animosity that has built up on his side. Remember that someone has been complaining to him the whole time, and he needs to let *you* know who is boss.

First, formulate the apology with your peers, and agree on exact boundaries for the discussion. If concessions are to be made on the business side, make sure the appropriate function is represented in the meeting. You are not expected to carry these decisions by yourself. Your job is to take the punches. As the Product Manager, however, you will be expected to commit fixes, so be prepared to do so.

Take this opportunity to shine among your peers. Make sure you let them know that you do not relish this sort of thing and that you are taking one for the team. Make them give you honest answers. You are the lamb for the slaughter, and everyone will be more than happy to serve you the last supper as long as they know they are not the ones to be sacrificed to the customer.

You have temporary absolute power. Make people work *for* you. It is amazing how quickly information you ask for will come once they realize they are off the hook for the meeting. Do not be afraid to act like the boss, and if someone is not cooperating, go to your executive, and let him or her know it.

The closer you get to the fateful meeting, the more frantic you should act. This is not far from the truth, because you will actually be on the edge. Find a balance between sounding frantic and looking like you are in control. The better this balance, the easier it will be for you to leverage the short-term, absolute power you have.

James avoided coffee that morning. It made him talk faster and sound jittery, even when he was not nervous. That day, he was very nervous and decided coffee wouldn't help. He had done his homework and been on calls with Sales, Engineering, Support—everyone, but God—for the past two weeks. They had run out of time, and his day of reckoning had come. The customer call was happening at one that afternoon.

The customer was a large, multinational financial institution. Moondoggie had worked the account for years before getting its first bite at the apple. It was a small installation that went smoothly and paved the way for larger and larger installations. The institution came to love Moondoggie's products and support. It was Moondoggie's largest single customer, always on the leading edge when deploying Moondoggie products and gladly participating in beta trials, providing references, and chairing the user group. The companies had become true partners.

However, this financial institution was still a customer. When something went wrong, the company expected it to be fixed and monitored SLAs carefully. There were regular reviews with the support team to ensure issues were being fixed. The directors of IT had Moondoggie's VP of Support on speed dial and were diligent in applying patches and fixes, but they expected to be serviced immediately and problems to be addressed fully. They were tolerant of glitches, as, over the years, they had learned that some problems just take time to fix. Still, they sometimes threw a fit.

One of Moondoggie's recent releases was problematic from the start. Scalability had been an issue, and James knew it but could do nothing to stop the release from going GA. He tried to limit the exposure by implementing a controlled-release program, intending to deploy the product only to the simplest of topologies and the smallest of customers until the first service pack to fix the issue. The company purposely kept the release out of the hands of large companies. The institution heard about it and insisted on deploying the product because of much-needed features. Lauren overrode James and authorized the release.

The financial institution deployed the product, which crashed its CRM system. Several weeks passed before a patch was developed. The VP of Support left Moondoggie in the meantime, and no one was liaising with the customer. The next call was to the VP of Sales, informing him that the institution was writing an RFP, with the intention of replacing Moondoggie everywhere.

The next few weeks were a living hell for James. He wanted to tell Lauren, "I told you so," but that would have been career-limiting. She was on the ropes for authorizing the deployment. In turn, she made life for her entire team a living hell by demanding daily updates and wreaking havoc with Engineering and getting in James's way.

Ultimately, they were given a week to fix the problem or get completely thrown out of the largest installation in the world, New York City. As of the day of the call, there was not a fix yet, and they were instructed to ask for another week. As the director of Product Management, Lauren was expected to deliver the bad news to the customer. She delegated it to James.

James booked a conference room for the day and locked himself in it. He brought in various Engineering and support personnel throughout the morning to review what he already knew backward. The last two weeks were nothing but this issue for him. He even knew what the fix was, but writing the code and testing would take time. He ate a light lunch alone while waiting for the call, staring at the Art Deco print on the wall. He had seen the picture, a wide-angle view of a boy fishing on the beach, many times in the conference room. Today the boy looked lonely and small.

The first person to walk in the room was the VP of Engineering, Rod. He was smart and soft-spoken, with a pragmatic view and over two decades of experience in the industry. He and James got along very well. Although everyone joining the call that day was under the gun, no one more so than Rod. As the head of Engineering, he considered it a personal blow to have such a large software release go so badly. Rod was even tempered and always smiling. He was not smiling so broadly that day.

The next three people to show up were from Support. Lea, the new VP of Support, was tall, skinny, and efficient. Her hair was cropped short, and she favored designer suits that were both fashionable and businesslike. She spoke clearly, with a no-nonsense attitude, and expected the same of everyone. She had received the brunt of the customer's ire and had taken over the position at a time when the issue came to a head. She was not a big fan of James or Rod, although she treated them with respect. In tow were the director of Tier 3 Support, Tommy, and the senior manager of Tier 3, Phil.

The last two people to come in were two of Rod's directors, Becky and Eric. Their development teams were responsible for the area of code with the issues. James opened his bridge ten minutes early. He was expecting the account manager, George, and his Sales Engineer, Sidney. They dialed in early at his request. It was a bit superfluous since they had all been on prep calls every day for the past week, so there was nothing more to be said. Purposefully absent were George's boss, the regional sales director, and the VP of Sales.

A caller beeped at the top of the hour, and James knew it was the customer. There were three attendees on their side in a conference room. James asked everyone to introduce themselves, starting with the customer. The CIO spoke first.

"Vogel Bryant, CIO," he said curtly.

"Ashley Merriweather, VP, Customer Care. My team is the main user of the product."

"Bruce Rogue, director of IT. I've been working with Tommy's team."

James thanked them and went around the table, including the sales team. He then laid out the agenda for the call.

"Per our last call, we have three agenda items today," he began. "First, review the status of the New York site to date. Second, discuss the plan to deploy the patch to the other affected sites. Third, discuss the long-term fix and the time lines for delivery."

James set up the agenda to start with the good news. The New York site had been running for a week without issues, so they were confident of the recent patch. Although there were other issues on the site, the root cause of the crash had been addressed, and he wanted to maintain focus on that. He also had a plan approved by both Engineering and Support for deployment to the other affected sites. They needed only a small maintenance window, which could be done at night, and they were ready to parachute one of Lea's best support Engineers to each site in turn.

"If you don't mind," Bryant, the CIO, bellowed abruptly, "I'd like to hear about the long-term fix first, James. I haven't heard anything from Ashley's team this week, so assume the patch works. I don't see any issues with deploying on the other sites, and Bruce is nodding his head in agreement."

So much for the good news.

"Sure, Vogel," James chirped, trying to sound enthusiastic. Rod signaled to ask whether James wanted him to take over, but James shook his head and smiled reassuringly. He wanted to get to the point. "We believe the patch is the correct fix but need to make sure it's robust. We'll need a week to complete it."

An awkward silence followed. When Vogel finally spoke, he sounded like he was trying to suppress anger but failing.

"So let me get this straight. You piddled around with this problem for three weeks while our CRM system limped along after you crashed it. Then you pointed fingers for another week before an Engineer even bothered to log into the system and then gave us half a dozen patches that didn't work. Two weeks ago, you told me we would have the permanent fix deployed in two weeks, which puts it at this Friday. Six weeks of lost business, and now you're telling me to wait another week?"

He inflated and embellished on the details, of course, to make his point. Lea wanted to set him straight on a couple of those, and James sensed that, so he spoke quickly.

"Yes, you're right, I apologize," James chimed in, looking at the speakerphone as if trying to hypnotize it. "We did have issues with the patches, and I'm sorry for the delays. We promised a fix by this

Friday, but we also want to make sure it's absolutely correct. The code is written, but the QA will take a week. The test bed includes all the topologies you use, and we want to run every possible contingency. I apologize. We'll need just a little more time."

He was grateful when someone else on the other side spoke. It was the VP of Customer Care.

"So, can we continue to run with this current patch?" Ashley asked.

"Yes," Lea responded, sensing James needed a break. "It's the final patch, as I understand, and there's no limit as to how long you can run with it. We do want to give you the final fix as soon as possible, though."

"And can you deploy the patch at the other sites now?" Ashley continued.

"Yes," Lea replied. "We're ready to send our team on-site as soon as you say."

"I'm saying it," Ashley fired. "Send them now."

"Absolutely," was the right answer from Lea. "He will be on-site in New York in the morning. I understand from recent discussions that you want us to follow with St. Louis, Chicago, and San Francisco, in that order."

"Fine," Ashley replied.

The rest of the discussion, to James's relief, was more tactical in nature. Bruce was interested in when the Engineer would be on-site so he could provide access and the schedule for the other sites. The CIO left the meeting when the discussion turned tactical, and that was further relief for everyone. The tone calmed somewhat.

The conversation meandered toward the root cause of the issue. Although they had sent e-mails explaining the problem in detail, Rod and his team were compelled to explain the root cause to Bruce and Ashley again. They also provided a detailed analysis of how it could be prevented in the future. At the ninety-minute mark of what had been planned as a one-hour call, everyone was spent. James wound down the call with some lighthearted remarks about the weather and a round of thank-yous. He had never been so happy to push the "End" button on the speakerphone.

It Is Not Paranoia When They Really Are Out to Get You

Get used to the idea that you have a target painted on your back.

Product Management is a unique function that conveniently puts you in the sights of anyone wishing to place blame. If an installation falls on its face, Sales, Presales, and Professional Services blame you. If the product is late, Engineering and Marketing blame you. If there are too many issues with a new feature or release, Support blames you.

There are plenty of schools of thought out there. The most common is that Product Management is ill defined or, perhaps, it is too broadly defined. No other function in a company touches so many areas and is perceived so differently by various people. The advantage of it is that you can touch so many things and influence so many functions. The disadvantage is that the breadth of your job definition and responsibility could arbitrarily change at any given moment.

Even in the most rigid and process-oriented organizations, it is difficult for a Product Manager to squeeze out of a situation where someone blurts out, "Isn't that a Product Management responsibility?"

See yourself as the General Manager, not a spreadsheet manager or a document manager. The more you see yourself as a business manager, the more you will act that way and, consequently, be seen as someone who knows the business side.

For a Product Manager, there is no such thing as being *too* business oriented. It actually is your job to keep reminding everyone that the whole point is to sell product. When someone says you are too sales oriented, take it as a compliment. The CEO is more likely to retain a person who is sales oriented.

Imagine yourself as owner of the business. The questions you would ask yourself and your subsequent behavior will greatly differ with that perspective, relative to if you simply saw yourself as an extension of Engineering. This is not arrogance or hubris. It is a matter of perspective.

As the owner of the business, you will discover that many things that worry people on a daily basis do not worry you as much because you are focused on bigger things: growing the business, market share, acquisition. Of course, you are not really going to be making these decisions, but, if you orient your mind-set to a business owner's perspective, your decisions and guidance to Engineering will reflect that mentality.

The New Widget May Leave the Customer Stranded

While innovation is welcome and rewarded, we must be keenly aware of innovation for its own sake. From one release to the next, there must be continuity of product features so that customers' perception is that they are getting both wonderful new features and preserving the ones they love.

Customers do fall in love with features, and they will let you know they are unhappy when you take away their favorite widget. There are two reasons why a customer objects to the change. The first is habit, and the second is business process. Both can be costly. If a customer has formed a habit around the feature, the users will object to the change because they will have to change their behavior. If retraining is involved with the new paradigm, this could translate to real dollars for the customer. When a customer builds its business process around your feature, he will have invested time and money into creation of the process, the implementation of the technology, and the training of the people. A new paradigm that impacts any of these can mean significant costs.

At times, there are ways to reframe customer mentality to the new paradigm. However, the bigger the customer, the louder the voice, and a small benign change may end up being a rip and replace of your product if mishandled. A flashing green light changing to a steady blue light may become a big deal for some customers.

Engineering's initiative to go to a new code base to make the product scale better, run faster, or become modern does not trump the value that the installed base places on the flashing green light. As the Product Manager, it is your job to understand the values that customers place on each feature and prioritize which ones can be reframed, substituted, or deprecated altogether.

In order to do this, you must have your fingers on the pulse of the customer. If the customer has built his business processes around the flashing green light, he will be harder to dissuade and more likely to react negatively to a change that does not fit those business processes.

For each new set of requirements, regardless of how small the increment from the previous release, ask these questions:

- Am I aware of the different uses that customers utilize my features for?
- Will this new feature impact existing features, and to what extent?
- Is this new feature going to benefit existing customers or bring in new customers?
- Is this new feature benefitting Engineering, Support, Marketing, or Sales? Does it sacrifice anything from the customer's perspective in order to benefit these groups?
- What is the cost-to-benefit ratio from the customer's perspective?

There are no absolute answers to these questions. The goal is to be aware of what the answers are and be prepared to live by the consequences. It is your job to inform the rest of the company of those consequences.

If changing the flashing green light to a steady blue light forces customers to retrain personnel, Engineering, Support, and Training teams must be aware that they will need to create new documentation, prepare for a higher volume of support calls, and develop new training courses as possible demands from the customer base. Marketing may need to understand that the product now features the competition's main color prominently on the interface. Sales may need to know that the new feature raises the product cost. It does not mean the company will not implement the new feature but that everyone understands the consequences of such a decision.

Part 4: Getting Through the Day

Today's Number One Is Different from Yesterday's

A good friend of mine once said he wished he could clone himself a few times so that he could handle the workload. I disagreed. You cannot throw bodies at a problem (even hardworking intelligent ones like my friend) and expect to get ahead. You throw bodies at something when you are having trouble keeping up.

The answer is not more, it is less. Prioritize, prioritize, and prioritize. Knock down the biggest problems first. There is a reason they are the biggest. Or take care of small issues that have the potential to become the biggest problems.

Although your priorities might be different from the next Product Manager, you each have to prioritize so as not to lose track of what's next. The best place to start is your boss. Know his or her priorities. Everyone will act like they are your boss and as though their needs come first. These premises are both wrong. Your boss is the only person you need to consider a boss, and his or her needs come first. Of course, your needs will reflect those of your boss. The point is that everyone else comes second.

Four things you can do right away are:

- Do not attempt to answer every e-mail; start with the ones your boss will really care about. You will find that the list narrows significantly.
- Cut your attendance to meetings and conference calls in half. If you have to, apologize in advance for leaving so that the others will be compelled to do your bits first. If they do not, it was not that important in the first place, and you'll be glad to leave.
- Take the weekend off.
- If all else fails, take a vacation day or two. You've earned it.

The reason there seems to be no end in sight is that THERE IS NO END. The work will be there tomorrow. We will use the well-known Urgency/Importance Matrix[1] in our illustration.

Figure 4. The task-priority matrix.

If you have done a good job of prioritizing, you will have ended up working on the items that fall into the two tactical quadrants: IMPORTANT-URGENT and NOT-IMPORTANT-URGENT. You know you have done a *great* job if you have also worked on the strategic quadrant: IMPORTANT-NOT-URGENT. What you want is to keep from working off the IMPORTANT-URGENT quadrant all the time, where you surely will be swimming against the tide. However, some things come into your view already in that quadrant. Working on tasks that are in IMPORTANT-NOT-URGENT keeps things in the IMPORTANT-URGENT quadrant to a minimum.

[1] Based on Stephen R. Covey's *The 7 Habits of Highly Effective People*, 1989.

In-Box ≠ Task List

Instead of having Outlook (or your favorite e-mail application) start up in the in-box, try making it start up in a view that shows your appointments and tasks as well. This global view puts you in a better position to prioritize activities for the day rather than tempting you to dive into the last e-mail that you received.

Starting with your in-box means you are using it as your task list, whether you think so or not. If you are to stay relevant and strategic, there should be something strategic you are working on daily.

Of course, the boss darkening your doorway will always take precedence, but few other things should. Where you start your day—or more to the point, what you use as your dashboard—is as important to starting the day right as exercise or other routines you employ to get prepared.

E-mail Is Not a Chat Room

E-mail has evolved from a tool of communication to a place where people hide. Although traveling at the speed of light, it is arguably slower to get anything done with e-mails today than with the paper memos of years past.

People misuse e-mails all the time. It has become a CYA tool. E-mail is meant to be a memorandum or a letter. It is meant to be somewhat of an official record of decisions made on behalf of the company. It is not a chat room. There is an app for that, and most companies welcome the use of Instant Messaging (IM).

The trouble is, with the proliferation of smartphones that allow e-mail, chat, and text messaging on one handheld device, the lines blur between these very different tools. Even though text messaging and IM can be saved, e-mail is still a more formal and official way of communicating.

E-mail has a time stamp embedded in it and an official log on the mail server. Chat and text might carry some of this metadata, but they are difficult to audit. This is by design because, again, they are meant to be casual and fleeting.

When you write an e-mail, assume that it will be catalogued by the receiver and that copies of it will exist forever. This should temper any impulse to express your emotion in the heat of the moment. It is a permanent record. An executive once advised me to sleep on an emotional e-mail before sending it. As a young Engineer, it made sense because I actually did end up writing a heated e-mail, which I consequently deleted after sleeping on it. Nowadays, I simply do not write them to begin with. If I get hot, I walk away from the PC.

People will judge you by your e-mails. As casual as we treat e-mails these days, it is surprising how much you will get judged by your e-mails. This is because everyone knows that it is still the most official form of communication. It is like signing in blood. Ever have someone pull out an e-mail you wrote months before to throw you under the bus?

Lastly, remember that many people judge or catalog the e-mail based on the subject line. Do not put casual or meaningless garbage in the subject, such as, "Thunderbirds are Go," or, "I Want this Back." If there is actual technical- or business-critical content in the e-mail, how is the receiver going to catalog it? Just like your signature, the subject will speak volumes to others.

Work Offline

When e-mails are coming in faster than you can process them, it becomes overwhelming, to the point of frustration. Accept the fact that you simply cannot keep up with e-mails. You have to prioritize, but you cannot do this when they are beeping in every few seconds.

First, turn off the e-mail alert. You know you are going to get one regularly, so why do you need a reminder?

Second, your in-box is NOT your to-do list. Do not treat it that way, or you will never feel in control.

Third, work offline. You will be better able to concentrate on a response when you are not distracted by the e-mail alert box lighting up every minute or the in-box counter increasing. This is particularly important when an e-mail response requires some research on your part. You want to be able to read documents, talk to or text people, and, yes, even generate more e-mail (without necessarily forwarding the original one) to support your research. There is something satisfying about clearing a dozen e-mails from the in-box without watching the counter go up, and watching the outbox counter go down when you reconnect. Yes, there will also be another dozen waiting to fill the in-box when you reconnect, but you weren't distracted by each one coming in, were you?

"But what if one comes in that really requires my attention?" you might ask. It is possible that it is more important or, more to the point, more urgent than the one you are working on right now, yes. Is it devastating to the business? If it were, someone would be following up with a phone call, a text, or, the old-fashioned way, showing up at your desk. The point is, if these latter three do not happen, the importance/urgency of that latest e-mail probably does not justify distracting you from the work you were already doing for someone else who also thought his e-mail was important and/or urgent.

Conference Calls Are a Waste of Time

Anyone who has ever told me they were so busy because they spend so much time on conference calls was telling me they were doing no work. Even with the best of multitasking skills, it is not effective to listen actively on a conference call while working on something at the same time.

The average audience's attention span is about twenty minutes. After that, you have to switch focus in order to reacquire the attention of the participants. I will grant that, sometimes, a participant is only needed for a portion of the call (say, thirty minutes), and they will typically spend the rest of the time doing something else. This is not multitaskingbecause you are no longer focused on the call, you are focused on whatever else you are doing. Or, are you? Isn't a part of you still listening for your name to be called on the conference call, even though the rest of the conversation is white noise?

Here is a bold idea: hang up when your bit is done. Knowing you won't be there for the entire call will force the participants to completely address the issues for which you are needed. Or dial in when the agenda calls for your participation. The work that you do the balance of that hour will be more focused and effective than having the conference call as white noise. Both of these tactics will also help you avoid the embarrassment of asking someone to repeat his question to you because you only rejoined the conversation when you heard your name called.

If you are spending the majority of your day on conference calls, how effectively are you doing all your other work? Can you really concentrate as well when there is conversation going on around you? Besides, why would you want to hear conversation that isn't relevant to your work?

Take Care of Yourself

When you are deep in the throes of your work, there is a tendency to let yourself go, especially with the hectic schedules we have. The demands on our time extend way beyond the traditional workday, thanks to the modern gadgetry that keeps us plugged in no matter where we are.

It might seem cool to have one of these gadgets orbiting your waist wherever you go, but realize that every one of them, from laptops to tablets to smartphones, serve the purpose of getting more work out of you for no more pay. This is not to suggest you turn off your smartphone or leave your laptop at work (although, would it kill you to do that once in a while?) but to temper your usage by creating a balance between life in cyberspace and life on earth.

Is today's high-tech software company little more than a dressed-up version of a third-world sweatshop? Have we come a long way from the factory-oriented thinking of the 1950s? Weren't these devices meant to allow us more flexibility in our work hours? You given a laptop so that you could do your work during nonbusiness hours, but doesn't that also translate into more flexible hours? It should, but the nature of the workplace has not really changed much from the factory-oriented days. We work the eight-hour day and go home to work another eight hours. And we are proud of it.

If the demands on us will not change—and I am pretty sure they will continue to escalate—then the best defense is a good offense. Take some time out, and do it on purpose. Create time for yourself, and make it sacred. Be it exercise, recreation, or hobby. Treat it like a meeting you are hosting—it is not an option for you to miss it. Put a strategy around it like you would any project: you research it, plan for it, and execute it.

Put Your Fingerprints on the Right Things

Whether you think so or not, you have the choice NOT to work on something. It is always easier to say yes and pick up yet another project. The most difficult thing is to say no and pass the thing along to the next in line.

The yes mentality comes from a couple of different sources.

- The new project, however benign or trivial it might be, could have the potential for growing into something that will boost your career. There is an even chance that it is just something that someone does not want because he or she has deemed it a dead end. Only you can determine that.

- The opportunity to excel or the mentality that "no job is too small for me to handle." The problem is, you become the dumping ground for stuff no one wants to work on.

- The problem is difficult, and you think you are the only one who can solve it. This is the peon in all of us crying out to become a hero. Do not go there unless you have determined that this is definitely one that will boost your career.

On Being a Road Warrior

As a Product Manager in high tech, you are expected to be on the road for a portion of your time. Conferences, speaking engagements, field enablement, partner meetings, and customer meetings are all part and parcel of the job. It is not glamorous.

Traveling can be the least enjoyable part of the job. It can certainly feel the least productive. Flight delays, long lines, and bizarre security protocols all contribute to the feeling that there must be a better way to stay connected to the field. Unfortunately, there is not.

If you want to get close to the field, to the business partner, and to the customer, you must be at handshaking distance. The all-too-familiar and credible studies about the amount of information lost by not being able to see a person have proven themselves over time. Even videoconferencing does not work, because there is an element of unrealism due to the fact that you are not really looking someone in the eye. There is no substitute for being in front of a person, especially if he or she is the decision maker. Customers love it when you go to see them. They feel important. Salespeople appreciate it when you visit their customers. It makes the Salesperson look influential.

Traveling does have its perks. Eventually, you will gain enough status on your favorite carrier to get preferential boarding, preferential check-in, and preferential security screening. Membership to lounges may be discounted or free of charge, in which case you can look forward to free drinks and free Wi-Fi. You will also get to meet new people, some of whom may be prospective customers or employers. All will certainly enhance your experience in one way or another.

One thing to take heart is the fact that most of the people you will see and meet are road warriors like you. Eventually you will learn to spot the nonprofessional traveler. You will likely ignore them or shake your head in disbelief at their unfamiliarity with travel protocol ("Why can't I carry my liter bottle of mineral water on the plane?"). The occasional/holiday traveler may even become a nuisance to you, as they inevitably slow down any process due to ignorance or apathy (they happen to be road warriors who are on vacation). There are ways to mitigate the pain.

Fewer flight legs mean saving time. Not only do you save time waiting around for your next flight, you also lower the risk of a missed or cancelled connection. A nonstop flight to your destination may mean the difference between spending an extra night or going home early. If you don't live near a hub, nonstops will be difficult, but you can still work to minimize the number of legs.

Strike a balance between a flight that is cheaper because it is at an odd time when no one wants to fly versus one that keeps you sane. If you are traveling to see a customer or business partner (also your customer), you should strive to be in good shape when you land and not jet-lagged from a red-eye.

Choose a hotel that is close to your meeting or centrally located among several meetings, especially if you are unfamiliar with the city, but not so expensive as to draw the boss's ire. Being late for a meeting due to unfamiliarity with traffic patterns or simply getting lost is not an acceptable excuse. Your professionalism as a representative of the company will go a long way toward establishing the proper first impression.

Try not to be outrageous with your rental car. Do not upgrade to the convertible until you have met the client and understand his or her nature. If it's an environmental group, get the smaller car. It also helps to get a sedan so that you will be prepared to give folks a ride to lunch or dinner. The more conservative your choice in vehicles, the less the attention will be on it and the more attention will be paid to your agenda.

International Travel

My resume describes me as "knowledgeable of and responsive to the cultural nuances of the international business world." This pretty much has to be true of you if you are to leave US shores. Even if you are going to a primarily English-speaking country, like South Africa, India, Australia, Hong Kong, the Philippines, and, yes, even the UK, it will serve you well to learn local customs when it comes to the business world. Do you give gifts? Do you stand when you present? Do you make hand gestures when you talk? How loudly do you speak?

Ideally you are accompanied by a local who can tell you. However, they may be reticent to apprise you for fear of offending you. Forget that. Ask him or her exactly how you should behave and what the customer or partner expects of you. Ask your colleague how you should dress, which colors are offensive, and whether a low monotone is preferable to a lively and loud voice. Is smiling a sign of something good or bad?

No matter what your title, you will likely be presented as someone of rank and certainly will be regarded with deference just because you came from corporate. Be aware that there is also an expectation that you can answer hard questions and that you are there because your company thinks this audience is important enough to warrant your presence.

Be humble. Americans are generally regarded as arrogant, so you may have to go out of your way to prove otherwise. This does not make you weak; it makes you look smart enough to have figured out the culture. Do not confuse self-confidence with arrogance. No one likes to see an arrogant person on their turf. If the particular culture you are visiting rewards humility, show that you are sensitive enough to conform. Exude confidence, but in a friendly way.

International travel exacerbates fatigue because of the length of time you spend on the plane and the time difference when you get there. There are tricks you can use to mitigate the jet lag. It starts with your choice of flight.

The most direct route helps. From the time you leave home, the wear and tear on your body starts. Connections add time and effort to your trip.

Try to arrive at your destination so that you have a half day or even a day to relax and recover. This is more difficult to do than you might think. The pressures of the job may dictate you leave at the latest time possible and arrive just in time. Consider that flights from the East Coast to London typically leave between five and ten at night and arrive between six in the morning and noon. If you leave on a Sunday evening, you could conceivably take an early enough flight and believe that the sleep you get on it will be enough so that you will be good for a meeting at half past nine after landing at six.

It took me several years of doing this before I decided it is folly and that my effectiveness in the meetings are greatly enhanced by arriving in the middle of the day before and having the afternoon to acclimate. The cost of an extra night at the hotel is worth it. Just because you have traveled across the ocean does not give you any excuses in the eyes of the locals. If you are meeting a customer, you are expected to be at your best.

Once you board a flight, it helps to think in terms of the time zone at your destination. I will start by setting my watch to that time zone and conducting myself on the flight as if I were already there. There are two variables in your circadian rhythms that have the biggest impact on jet lag: sleeping and eating cycles.

The formula is simple: do what the people are doing at your destination, throughout your flight. If they are sleeping, you should be as well. If they are eating, so should you. Of course, the airlines do not adhere to this schedule. You will typically get served a meal upon takeoff and another upon landing. Depending on the length of the flight, there may be more in between. If one of these meals does not line up with your destination schedule, skip it. Even the meals in first or business class are not really worth the loss of sleep. If your destination dictates you sleep at the beginning of the flight and miss the meal, you can get something at the airport before departure. The flight attendants are usually nice enough to give you something in the middle of the flight. It may not be the hot meal they served four hours earlier, but you will survive.

When you arrive and it's daytime, do not give in to the temptation to take a nap. This is why you set yourself to follow the local cycle while you were still on the flight. Even though airplane sleep is nowhere near the rest you get in a proper bed, you should have had enough to carry you through the day and get to bed at the right time. Try doing a short, light workout at the hotel. Even better, tour the city on foot. A little bit of activity helps you recover from the jet lag faster. A good friend and colleague advised me to get exposed to the sun as a way of combatting jetlag. Even on a cloudy day, it's better to be outside.

Me, a Workaholic?

I think everyone will agree that today's office worker is an allegorical factory worker, even the proverbial sweatshop worker. The latter is probably more appropriate, as we can see by the amount of time we spend on the laptop, the desktop, the tablet, and the smartphone, e-mailing, IMing, talking—sometimes all at the same time.

I am a workaholic. There is no question about that. If I retired today, I would be looking for a new job tomorrow. I would be working at something.

I can turn anything into intense (and sometimes stressful) work. You name it: gardening, woodworking, bowling, golf, scuba diving, car washing, and so on. That may sound amusing, but it underpins my success in my career—and some of the failures.

Being a workaholic basically means you like running on a treadmill. It is completely tactical. Running on a treadmill may mean you are giving your heart exercise, but it does not necessarily translate to good overall health. Failure to develop a strategy (cardio exercise, plus diet, plus lifestyle) may mean you are really busy and satisfying the need to be productive, but, you're not doing yourself or the company a huge favor by losing track of *why* you're doing what you're doing. The question is, to what end are you doing it?

There's an aphorism I like to paraphrase that summarizes the gap between strategic and tactical:

> *When you're up to your waistline in alligators, it's hard to remember why you wanted to drain the pond in the first place.*

Prioritizing your tasks every day forces you to take perspective and helps you work on the things that are truly important. A friend of mine used to have a policy of not looking at new e-mails until after lunch. His logic was that, most of the time, e-mails are broadcasted to a number of people in the hope that someone will respond. Someone usually does, but it doesn't have to be you.

The constant blocking and tackling you have to do can contribute to your loss of perspective. There is the temptation to just get the ball off your hands because you know that other balls are going to be thrown your way. You do not have to catch them all.

Whatever intimidates you the most or seems the most complex is probably the first big thing you should tackle that day. Do not procrastinate. There is satisfaction that comes with completing a task, so, sometimes we may postpoine starting one that we know will take some time to complete. We gravitate to the ones with the potential for immediate gratification. Prioritize, prioritize, prioritize. Start the important task and just tell yourself you are going to get it going. You will be surprised at how many times it actually gets finished in the same day, or at least sooner than you think.

Sometimes the toughest thing to do is just get started. In order to get your day kick-started, do the simplest thing that contributes to the bigger task. Chunk up the big job into bite-sized pieces, and the enormity of the task will shrink. Eat the elephant one bite at a time.

Take the Weekend Off

A colleague of mine once asked me if I worked on the weekends. My answer, "Doesn't everybody?" evoked a look of pity. I proceeded to complain about the people who would continue to e-mail me through the weekend, expecting an immediate answer. I could not just leave them alone, could I? His answer: "No, but you can make him think you did and deliver the results first thing Monday. Who's going to die if you take the weekend off?"

His advice was brilliant. It starts with simply replying to the offending party that you will get back to them first thing Monday. Even if you finish the work five minutes after you send that reply, wait until Monday morning to send it back. No, really.

Sound duplicitous? Think of it as conditioning yourself and your constituents to regard your weekend as your time. The exception? Your boss. Do not make him or her wait longer than necessary. This book is, after all, about your survival.

You've still completed the work, but, have conditioned the world to respect your weekend. The alternative conditions them in the opposite direction: that they can abuse your personal time.

If you answer one e-mail by midnight on Friday, two more will need an answer in the same timeframe next week, and so on until you find yourself complaining to your boss that you have been working sixty- or seventy-hour weeks and get no respect, and so on. Empower yourself.

I've found that the work *does* get done, and funny enough, no one has died yet due to my answering an e-mail that comes in after dinner on Friday the following Monday.

There is a Wrong Way to Take Vacations

An out-of-office alert stating that you are on vacation does not mean you are. Is your vacation a result of having too many vacation days accrued (invoking the wrath of HR), or is it due to a real desire for respite—a time to recharge your batteries? You have to create the environment for a proper vacation.

- Leave your laptop home (this is the hardest part). There is a certain amount of separation anxiety that you will inevitably experience, like a part of you is being cut off. It lasts until the airplane door closes, and then a sense of relief comes over you as you realize there is nothing you can do about it now.
- Leave your smartphone home if people at work normally would call you on it (this is the second hardest part).
- Go for more than a week. It might take you three days to get work off your mind, so a seven-day vacation is really only four days at best. Make it ten days, and you will have been on vacation for a week.

- Go where people think blackberries and apples are only fruits, web is something that spiders make, and galaxy is an astronomical term.
- Have a goal for your highly driven, goal-oriented, type-A brain. Learn to scuba dive, treat your significant other like royalty for the entire vacation, find every species of flora or fauna in the local guide book, get more than eight hours of sleep a day, distinguish different varietals of wine, take pictures of the setting sun, etc.
- Keep the out-of-office alert simple: "I'm on vacation until [date]. I will have no access to e-mail. Please bother these other people (that you list at the bottom) during my absence."

Part 5: Your Career

James got home late again. It was not the hour that was concerning Ellie, it was the way he looked. He seemed more worried than usual the last few weeks. There was a time when he said he forgot all about work as soon as he walked in the door. It seemed now he had brought his work in the door with him.

He walked in as she was taking the baby upstairs. She had plastic-wrapped a plate for him and left it on the middle shelf of the fridge with a note that said, "Do not exceed 3 min ☺," meaning no more than three minutes in the microwave. He could hear her upstairs, trying to put the kids to sleep as he followed her directions and then started eating. She came down as he was halfway through his casserole and toying with it.

"What's up?" she asked cautiously. She read him like a book.

"I'm not getting paid enough for this, Elle, I swear."

As if suddenly remembering something, he stopped, got up to kiss her, and then continued with his tirade. "I'm not sure if I'm just not getting through to them or if they're deliberately trying to slow things down."

Ellie knew "them" was a reference to Engineering. A former programmer herself, she knew the lingo, the process, and the people.

"What happened?" was all she had to ask, and James went on for twenty minutes. Then a revelation came to him. He was not really complaining so much about Engineering as he was about the company. He was no longer happy there.

There was a time when he would be willing to leave a job at a moment's notice if something did not feel right to him. Back then, of course, there was no Julia or Jonah, and he had the luxury of falling back on Ellie's job to support them both. Now it was all different. The decision for Ellie to stay home was difficult but the right one. It also meant he had to be careful about making job decisions at the drop of a hat.

Ellie could not help wondering if the time for James to leave Moondoggie had come. The company had been good to him, no doubt. He came in with a wave of new Product Managers as part of the change in direction the company was taking.

They were supposed to take the product into the twenty-first century and change the way the whole industry looked at high-tech software. That was five years before, and although they were successful in turning around the product, they did not exactly make the impact envisioned by the new CEO.

On the other hand, the company became a success on the sales side, and James enjoyed the fruits of his labor in a different way—via his bonuses. As the company grew, management changed. The director who hired him moved on and was replaced by a younger, more ambitious, and politically oriented boss.

Although Laura seemed to like him, it was clear that she and James did not see eye to eye on many product issues. She was a micromanager, which everyone hated, but James did not mind. She gave him plenty of latitude but sometimes threw him under the bus. She had a tendency to take empowerment away from her team, which annoyed many people. She seemed to have many arguments with her direct reports. James realized she was not the kind of boss he wanted to have. She was not someone from whom he could learn how to be a good manager.

"I hate to say this, Ellie," he said in between bites, "but I think Laura might be bad for me."

Someone to Blame

A Product Manager's job is never finished. You answer to a multitude of masters, and none of them are ever really satisfied. If any one of them is happy, the others are not. The sales team thinks you are not rolling product out quickly enough, the marketing team thinks you are not giving them enough material to adequately market the product, and Engineering thinks you are pushing them too hard and that your time lines are unreasonable.

You have to be sensitive to all of these, because you are the focal point for all these functions. If anything goes horribly wrong, you will get the blame. As I read on a T-shirt once, "I'm not saying it's your fault; I'm saying I'm going to blame you."

At any point in the day, someone is throwing you under the bus. The good news is that you will not be fired for these small things because someone has to do the job. The bad news is that you will not be fired for these small things because someone has to do the job.

If you are lucky, you will hear just how unhappy people are with you. This is better, as it will put things in perspective. You cannot act on something you are not aware of.

You've heard people talk about getting a life, meaning outside of work. It is no more important than as a Product Manager. You have to get a hobby or devote yourself to your family, church, or golf course so that you can derive happiness through those means. At the end of the day, you are reenergizing yourself for the onslaught of the next day at work.

Fore!

The adage about golf being a path to success because all successful businessmen play golf seems trite. It is true that, more often than not, executives like to play golf. It gives them a reason to hang out with other decision makers like themselves.

This is not about playing golf. It is about being out there with the right people. It can be an industry association meeting, a road race, or an off-Broadway show. Consider it a necessary evil. Get access to people you may not normally have access to. Ideally it is an environment where you can comfortably approach people. It is not always about vertical advancement. It can be about getting help to get your job done.

"I thought you said you didn't play golf," Marcus said.

"No, I didn't say that." Sue looked up. "I said I didn't WANT to play. Actually, there was a time when I played every day. I played on my high-school team." She smiled. "We won the state championship. Played in college, too. "

"You know these guys aren't that good, Sue." Marcus looked worried and then got to the point. "We can't win, but we can't make it look like we're trying to lose either. Their egos won't permit that."

"I see. So don't outdrive them, and shank one or two into the woods," she said.

"Blow a four-footer by once in a while," he suggested with a smile.

"And take two strokes to get out of the sand," she finished. "Will I have to worry about them giving me advice? I really hate that."

"Yeah, they might. But don't hesitate to give ME advice." He winked. "I could use it."

Marcus was an up-and-coming Account Executive, which is what Matador called its sales reps. He had worked at H-P, Ricoh, and some small networking companies before joining Matador. He was young, energetic, and charismatic. He had a bright smile, and his light brown hair was thinning in spots you would not expect for someone his age.

He was the only AE of his class at Matador to achieve quota his first year and was earning a good reputation. Sue first worked with him on a seven-figure deal for a multinational bank that required special development on their workhorse 3000 series. It was three weeks' worth of development and about six months' worth of testing that she managed down to three months. He blew his number away that year. The next time he was in the office, he insisted on taking her to dinner and gave her two tickets to a ball game.

That was then, and this is now. Now he was courting a manufacturing firm with seven sites and asking for two levels of redundancy. The CIO and his right-hand man, the VP of IT, were avid golfers, and Marcus had originally set up this round with his

SE, Jon. When Jon got sick, he asked Sue to join him. She had been on several calls with the VP before, and they were more than happy to have her. Most customers love the idea of dealing directly with the Product Managers. It made them feel special.

Sue did as she said she would on the round, to Marcus's delight. They discussed business for about five minutes, and the rest was about the CIO and his passion for scuba diving. He had spent three weeks on a liveaboard in the Caribbean. Sue had no idea what a liveaboard was and suspected Marcus didn't either, but both nodded and chirped with interest.

At the end of the round, nothing more was said about the deal. The only clue Sue had that they had done something right was when the CIO said he would cut his trip to Seattle short and asked if Marcus could come a day earlier than their previously arranged meeting in two weeks. He wanted a more extensive demo.

The Company

Let's face it, most of us are working within a company culture that someone has set, and there is little we can do to change it.

The first point I will make is that if you can't stand the heat, get out of the kitchen. Do not try to change the recipes or tell the chef how to do his job. The job is tough enough without having to suffer through a culture that gets on your nerves. If it gets too hot, you have the option of leaving.

There is, of course, the practical side of things. You cannot be expected to jump companies on a trial-and-error basis for culture, nor can you expect to find the perfect company culture.

There is no ideal culture. There are sadly few examples of cultures that people think are ideal: Apple, SAS, Google, pre-Carly Hewlett-Packard, eBay, and so on, where the culture was embraced by all and seen as benchmarks for the industry.

The rest fall under the category of a culture that you can live with. This is what has become of the tech industry. Depending on where you are in your career, there will be a different way to approach the question of whether the culture will work for you or not.

Let us take our two Product Managers, for example.

Sue is a relatively new Product Manager, and she came into the job within the same company, rising through the Engineering ranks. In her previous company she was an engineer. Matador is the first company she has worked for as a Product Manager and been exposed to the culture and politics at that level.

Although she accepts the company culture, she is starting to see cracks in the armor and has come to realize that her style is not conducive to heavy politics that are rampant within the company. She is more at home in a culture that encourages the type of open— if not sometimes combative—style that she thrives in. She would be more at home in a smaller company closer to a start-up than a mature company, where she can shine as a participant in the development process and emerge as a leader when necessary.

She is more at home dealing with peers rather than politicking to the executives. She is comfortable at Matador because she knows everyone and how to work with them. She is, however, starting to realize that her career ambitions are being limited by the fact that she is not comfortable with the level of politics necessary to thrive in the company. She may be overlooked or even dismissed as nothing more than an Engineer type, even though she has demonstrated leadership ability equal to her bosses. Her often absent boss is not helping either. His style is to be completely hands-off, but Sue needs guidance. She is not comfortable paving her own path when faced with so many possibilities. At this point, a manager more concerned with her career would serve her well.

Matador is not optimal for her for these two reasons: politics and an absentee boss.

James has been a Product Manager for close to ten years, although he has only been with Moondoggie for a couple of years. He has worked for large and small companies alike and is closer to a pure business manager. He has never worked as an Engineer but understands the development process, the lingo, and the Engineer's mentality.

He has learned to work with the company culture, even though there are a few things he would like to fix. The company seems focused on the tactical and is very much Engineering driven. He and his fellow Product Managers are continually questioned on the strategy, and he repeatedly has to put his foot down and declare his job function. He wants to be taken for his word, but many of the Engineers were there during the company's start-up phase and were always part of all business decisions, as is prevalent in start-ups.

The problem for James is that the company is taking a long time getting out of that mode. Moondoggie is now a medium-sized company but still behaves like it is operating out of the founder's garage. The good thing is that James gets a lot of cooperation, as long as he can justify the request. His frustration stems from the fact that he can see opportunity for growth, yet even the executives seem reluctant to take on these opportunities because they, too, are stuck in the mode of pleasing one customer at a time and customizing to a painful degree.

James's boss is also getting in his way because she is in his face on everything and will not let him make a decision without approval. She thinks she is helping him and does not realize that her hovering is suppressing his creativity. She also does not understand that he must be allowed to work the system on his own, as opposed to her always helping him along.

The best culture for James is one where a Product Manager is responsible for a particular P&L and held accountable for it. He loves to be with Salespeople and customers. He is best when he is on a podium at a conference or in front of a customer—always surrounded by people. He is least comfortable in a setting where Engineers are asking his opinion on technology decisions, which he thinks of as their jurisdiction. He prefers to talk directly to someone, rather than through e-mail. He can close deals.

Ideally the company he goes with is more sales focused than Moondoggie. James can handle politics well, and he needs to have strong business analysts that effectively shield him from the constant battering of Engineering. He needs to have a boss who is hands-off and provides help only when asked. He needs the challenge of a revenue number to hit. He may never go to Sales, but he likes being close to that process.

For these reasons—the start-up mentality and his hovering boss— Moondoggie is the wrong company culture for James.

Find a Mentor

No matter how independent and self-made you are, you have the basic psychological need for validation. We all have the need to check in with someone who can provide us with data points that will tell us whether or not we have strayed from the path or with an outright plan to get us where we want. As Product Managers we need mentors.

Who is guiding you? Are you learning about your craft daily? Did you get that MBA and decided that was the end of learning? To be sure, we learn something new every day at work, but wouldn't it be more to your advantage to have some extra coaching?

I have kept up with some of the smartest people I have met in business. I have become very good friends with some of them and, to this day, still learn from them. Some things I have learned I continue to use. They have become universal truths in my life.

Your mentor does not have to be your direct manager. In many cases, it is an advantage if he or she is not. You have more freedom to discuss things. Your conversations do not have to be loaded, and you can explore possibilities from a broader perspective.

Although it helps if your mentor is in the same business, because he or she will be able to understand the nuances of your issues, they do not have to be. Someone completely outside of your line of work may provide you with the out-of-box thinking you may need from time to time. The advantage is that he or she does not drink the same Kool-Aid you do.

This person does not have to be more senior either. A lot of wisdom can be taken from someone who is less experienced but has a personality or attitude that makes them successful in their own right.

At the end of the day, a mentor will help provide you with the order that you will need in the chaotic life that we all know in the high-tech industry. They are sounding boards whose interest is your success. We spend so much time in the trenches that we may not always be aware of where we are going. That is the most valuable thing a mentor can offer: which way to point the rudder.

Sue liked talking to Walter. He was a grumpy old man she had met in a previous company, and both ended up working for Matador. He was very smart but so brutally honest that even he admitted he could not be in management. He neither loathed nor aspired to be in management. He was happy as a developer and was great at his job. He also liked and respected Sue—a fact she thought was a pretty rare combination for Walter.

Walter was in the lab testing a module. Sue was seated a few feet away, playing with a new motherboard when he noticed she had stopped working altogether and was staring at him.

"What's up, Susan?" he asked without looking up. "Something on your brain wanting to come out?"

"Walt," she began slowly, "where do you think the company's headed?"

His response was inevitably abrupt. "To the highest bidder," he said flatly, as if completely sure.

"What? Have you heard something I haven't?" she asked.

"You know everything I do," he said. "We're in a niche market. We are the eight-hundred-pound gorilla, but it's still a niche. I have to believe there are bigger fish out there ready to gobble us up."

"For what? The technology? The customer base?" she asked.

"All of the above," he replied. "Look, of the players in our space, there are really only a handful that do what we do. The rest put our functionality in their products because they have to. It makes sense for one of those bigger guys to buy someone in our niche and stop pretending they know how to do what we do."

"Why now?" She decided to test him.

"We're viable, debt-free, and the aforementioned gorilla." He winked.

"So are you going to stick around?" she asked.

"Until they kick me out, dear sister," he said. "Unlike you, I no longer have bigger ambitions than where I am now. You need to spread your wings, Sue. The only way to do that is leave. I'm afraid this place is a dead end for you."

Sue had a hard time with that one. On the one hand, Walter articulated something that was in her gut. On the other, it bothered her that she would have to leave. She liked the technology and the people she worked with. She liked the leadership, for the most part. Walter was right, though: her chances for advancement were slim. It was time to do some thinking.

Your Boss Can Make or Break You—Choose Wisely

You never really know how your boss is going to be until you have been working with him or her for a while. The interview process tells neither of you much about the other in terms of whether you will get along in the long run.

Although the boss is still the boss and you have to do what he tells you at the end of the day, in this industry, it is accepted practice to treat your relationship with your boss as a partnership rather than the traditional master-servant hierarchy.

Learn what your boss's style is AND understand what YOUR ideal is in terms of a boss's style to see if the two match.

- Level of involvement in your activities: hands-off or micromanagement?
- Decision making: does your boss decide for you, or with you?
- Willingness to be your mentor: not what's good for the team (i.e., your boss) but what's good for YOU.
- Air cover: when the going gets tough, does he stand in the line of fire for you?
- Promotion: does he care about your next career move, and is he helping you get there?

Sue was dragging. The morning's meetings had drained the energy from her. Another delay on the release that seemed to be of concern to no one, more useless meetings, fighting among the Engineering leads…it seemed to have no end.

She took a bite of her sandwich that had been waiting at her desk. It tasted stale. Joe would be back from lunch by now. She decided to catch him, as he usually did not schedule meetings right after lunch. It had something to do with not being as alert because of his food settling. She knew he just used the time to catch up on personal e-mails and update his social-media pages.

Directors at Matador got to sit in bigger cubes, with taller walls, and about three times the real estate of a normal cube. They even had sliding doors made of translucent plastic that gave the illusion of privacy, but you wouldn't dare hold a private conversation behind them. They were still cubes.

Joe Mirage always left his plastic door open because he told everyone he had an open-door policy. Of course, he was always off at a meeting with one of the execs or something, so the open door really led to nothing.

He was there, as she had predicted, picking at his nails and staring at his screen. He was positioned so that someone standing at the door to his fake office could not see his screen, but, out of the corner of his eye, he could see you.

He clicked "ESC" when Sue appeared at the door.

"Hey, Sue," he said. His voice was always even, friendly, and gave the impression he was glad to see you. "How goes?"

"Need to talk to you about the delay in R5. This is the second time in two weeks. What are we going to do?" She sat down, deflated.

"Yeah, I've already escalated to Randy. Engineering has some nerve."

It did not give her any comfort that the CEO was now involved. He would not do anything active. He would just make some statement about execution and time to market, assure Joe that Engineering was on the hook, and move on. It was not his problem. That is what the executives who report to him were paid to do. It would be up to Product Management to deal with the fallout with Sales and, at the same time, continue to drive something out of Engineering.

"You know, it's really QA causing the slip. They say the original estimate is null and void because we changed the scope. That's bullshit, and they know it. We added five lines of code, Joe." Her voice raised a little, and she caught herself.

He nodded reassuringly. "I got it, Sue. Believe me, I called a meeting with Frank in about a half hour. I'll give him hell. Make him call out Rebecca and get her to change the estimate."

"Why don't YOU call out Rebecca? Aren't you peers?" she wanted to say but thought better of it. It was so like Joe to avoid confrontation with his peers. He wanted to get along with all of them. She doubted he would give Frank, the VP of Engineering, the hell he had promised. He would just tell him, in the most politically correct way, how he disagreed with the QA estimates and ask if he could do him a favor and please bring it down a little for the sake of time to market and so he would not get in trouble with Randy...kiss, kiss, kiss. He would cover his ass so that when Angel, the VP or Product Management, asked him whether he talked to Frank, he could say, "Yes, I gave him hell."

He turned back to his screen and mumbled something about his calendar being full that afternoon. Sue was being dismissed, so she mumbled a "thanks" and shuffled off.

"Leave it with me," he shouted after her. "I'll take care of it."

Sue did not like the direction the company was going. She had been part of it since the start-up days. Now that they were growing up, the things that had attracted her to Matador were disappearing and being replaced by things she could not understand, like some of the people.

Her old boss, Rob, used to run the Product-Marketing and Product-Management teams. Product Management was taken from him, Joe was hired as the Product Management director, and they were put under their own VP. It made sense to have two different teams; they were growing in size and scope. She just could not align to the way Joe operated. He seemed to be more concerned about his relationship with the CEO and the VP of Engineering than running the team.

Sue appreciated a hands-off style, but she did need direction SOME of the time. Joe seemed to show up only when he had a problem or when one of his direct reports appeared to have screwed up.

The changes in Engineering also made it harder for her to get things done. Where she used to be able to go directly to a developer and get him or her to just add in some code on the side, they now directed her to a manager, who would scrutinize the request and make Sue document it. As a result of increased bureaucracy, some of her favorite Engineering colleagues left.

Sue brought this up with her boyfriend, Alex, at dinner one night. She wanted a somewhat objective perspective. She thought she was just being picky or inflexible. Alex, a developer at an Internet start-up, suggested she might be on to something.

"If people are jumping ship," he quipped, "you might want to check for leaks."

Think Two Jobs Ahead

Career self-help advisers have been telling us to plan ahead. When I started working, the idea of having a one-, five-, and ten-year plan was in vogue. Why a twenty-two-year-old would care about ten years hence, or even five, is still beyond me. Now older and wiser, I think I did a pretty good job of winging it.

Actually, I did have a plan. I just did not write it down. Could I have done a better job if I had? This becomes a matter of personal preference. At the time, I was happy to have long-term and short-term goals that I articulated in my head, and since there were not that many, I figured I could remember them without having to write them down. For an Engineer, I certainly was not as detail oriented about my career steps as I was with my Engineering design work.

In the last few jobs, I became more acutely aware of the advantages of careful planning. My goals have not changed, but I've added a few more steps in between. My personal situation has changed significantly since I was twenty-two, which necessitates some rethinking every now and then.

One of the most useful strategies I have come to employ is focusing on the next job. It seems almost treacherous to one's employer to be thinking about it, but it does help you focus on your own strategy. Frankly, there is no real loyalty to the employee anymore. You have to look out for number one.

The next job could be in the same company or a different one. To you, the professional manager, it should not matter. There is a level of comfort knowing the company, the people, and the business, but there is also the potential for learning in a different company or a new line of business.

Either way, think of the next job. Thinking two jobs ahead would be even better. This will truly focus your attention on doing the right things today to meet those next two goals.

You may have to choose certain aspects of the job according to how relevant it is to the future of the company. Product Management is not a straightforward or one-dimensional job.

You have to choose the things that will enhance your value to the team and to the company while doing something that is of interest to you. However, not all interesting things add value to your resume or to the company. You may have to decide to forego something interesting in favor of something that gives you visibility and credibility with people who make decisions (or influence those who do) in hiring.

It will not come very often, but you will have moments when the stars align and everything is in your favor. These are the moments when you feel it was worth the struggle and all the darts you had to take in the back.

It will come. Two important things to remember: (1) learn to figure out when it is coming, and (2) take full advantage of it.

Have you ever seen that cartoon where a crane has a frog halfway in his mouth? Although you cannot see the frog's upper half, he is using his front legs to choke the crane. The caption reads, "Never ever give up." Well, my Product Manager friend, you are the frog.

The Last Word

We have now looked at Product Management from different perspectives.

In Part 1, we focused on the job itself. We discussed the foundational elements of every high-tech Product Manager's position.

In Part 2, we looked at your relationships. We looked at your relationships and how to improve upon them.

In Part 3, we moved on to the business side. We turned our attention to understanding how the business side works.

In Part 4, we discussed some tips and tricks of getting through the day.

In Part 5, we focused on your career.

Product management can be a different job, depending on whether one is looking from the Sales or the Engineering side. There are also different types of Product Managers, but as we have seen, they all have one common goal: the right requirements.

We have also seen how a Product Manager's relationships can affect his decisions, performance, and the way he is viewed by the company. We now also understand that Product Management is a career path that can come from different disciplines and lead to a variety of exciting things.

Finally, we followed a pair of Product Managers with vastly different personality types, backgrounds, and styles of managing. They also differ in their ultimate objectives for what an ideal position entails.

Sue packed the last box, or so she thought. Her home office looked like a warehouse, with boxes neatly stacked by size and shape. She opened the bottom drawer of her desk and discovered that it was still full. It was her junk drawer, where things that were not quite ready for the trash found themselves until a day like this. She was so tired of packing that she felt like dumping the whole thing into a garbage can and never looking back.

A piece of plastic caught her eye. Her badge from the Product Manager conference in Vegas. She remembered her friend, James "GQ" from the East Coast and the ridiculous sessions they had attended. She flipped her phone open and looked for his contact. She opened a text session.

"Hey, James Herrera. It's Sue Lam, formerly of Matador, Inc. Remember the conference in Vegas?"

She put the phone down and started digging through the drawer, tossing most of the contents into an overflowing garbage can. The phone buzzed as she was tossing out a drink koozie from a defunct Internet company and a handful of pens from various software companies.

"Sue Lam! Wow! It's been a while. So you've moved on?"

"Yes," she replied, "well, still moving. My boyfriend and I both found jobs in Seattle. I start in two weeks. Network optimization start-up. What's new with you?"

"As it happens, I'm moving on, too. Not by choice."

"Sorry."

"Not at all. Didn't realize how miserable I was till I got laid off. The bad feeling lasted all of ten secs. Partly because the package was pretty good. My wife was glad, too. She says I've been a douche the past few months. Now I get to be Mr. Mom till I find something."

"Quality time with the kids. That can't be bad. Good luck on the job hunt," she replied.

"Interview tomorrow with big telecom company," he wrote. "Don't want to name them in case I jinx myself."

"Excellent. Let me know where you land. Stay in touch, GQ."

A smiley-face emoji came back.

www.ingramcontent.com/pod-product-compliance
Lightning Source LLC
Chambersburg PA
CBHW041152050326
40690CB00001B/449